Macramé Craft

STYLISH KNOTTED AND CROCHETED DECORATIONS, JEWELRY, AND ACCESSORIES

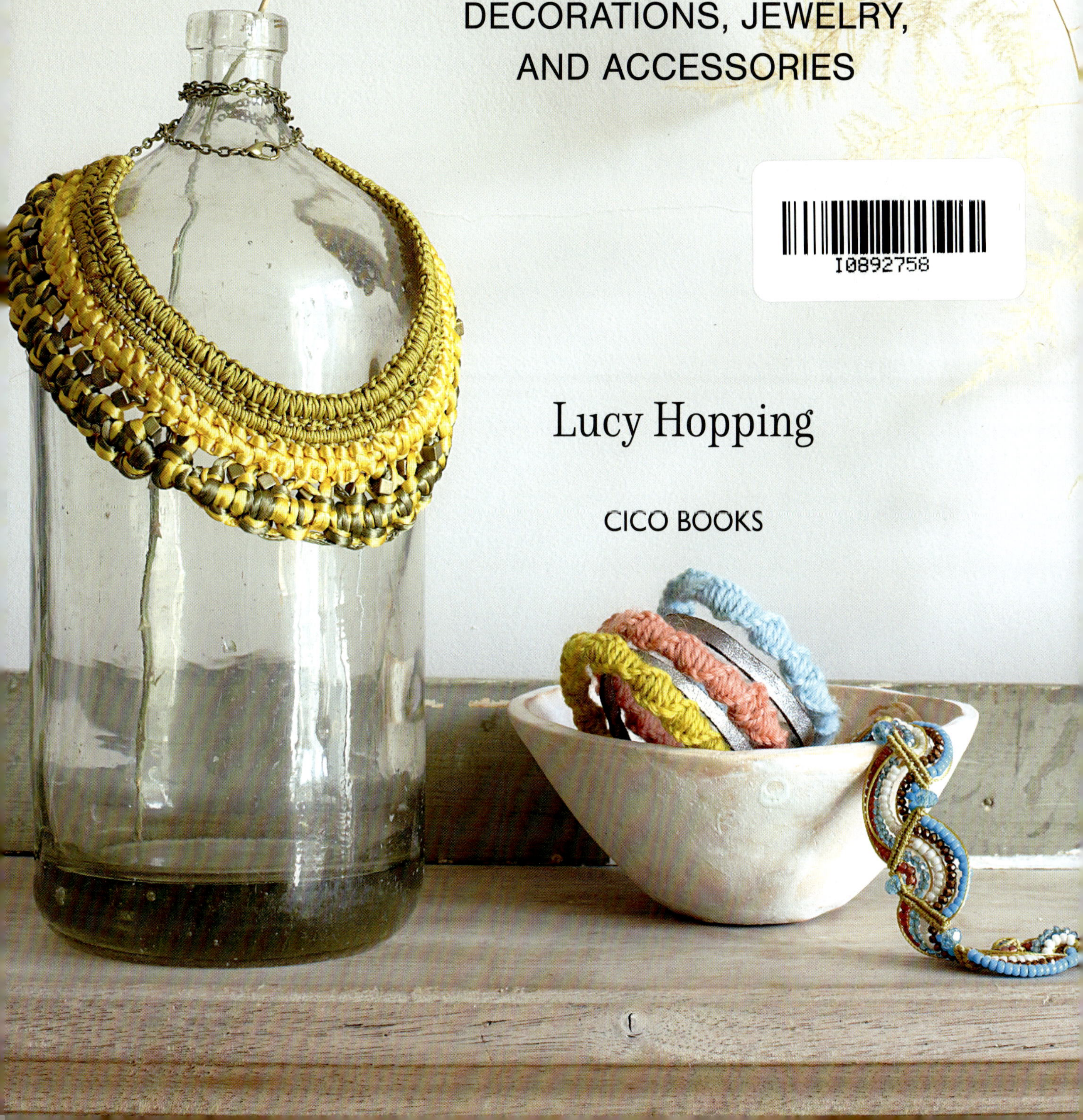

Lucy Hopping

CICO BOOKS

This edition published in 2025 by CICO Books
An imprint of Ryland Peters & Small Ltd
20–21 Jockey's Fields 1452 Davis Bugg Road
London WC1R 4BW Warrenton, NC 27589
www.rylandpeters.com
Email: euregulations@rylandpeters.com

First published in 2016 as *Macramé Jewelry & Accessories*

10 9 8 7 6 5 4 3 2 1

A CIP record for this book is available from the British Library.
US Library of Congress CIP data has been applied for.

ISBN: 978-1-80065-470-9

Printed in China

Editor: Marie Clayton
Designer: Elizabeth Healey
Photographer: Jo Henderson
Illustrator: Louise Turpin
Stylist: Luis Peral-Aranda

In-house editor: Anna Galkina
Art director: Sally Powell
Head of production: Patricia Harrington
Publishing manager: Penny Craig
Publisher: Cindy Richards

The authorised representative in the EEA is
Authorised Rep Compliance Ltd.,
Ground Floor. 71 Lower Baggot Street,
Dublin, D01 P593, Ireland
www.arccompliance.com

MIX
Paper | Supporting responsible forestry
FSC® C008047

Contents

Introduction

Macramé is the latest ancient craft to make a comeback and in this book we hope to inspire and excite you with 35 exciting jewelry and accessory projects made with a wide range of macramé techniques. With such a variety there is one to suit any mood, occasion, or outfit!

Macramé is believed to have originated in the 13th century, when Arabian weavers began knotting the excess threads from their woven fabrics into intricate patterns. This spread to Spain when the Moors invaded, and then throughout Europe. Sailors also soon adopted the technique to decorate items during the long months at sea. The craft came to a head during the Victorian times—no home was left unadorned, and complicated doilies and table cloths covered every available surface. Women were also encouraged to create beautiful knotted trims and laces for their clothes. The 1970s brought another resurgence in popularity for macramé; children made friendship bracelets whilst the parents decorated their homes with plant pot holders, statement chairs, and complex wallhangings!

But now it's time to bring macramé into the 21st century! If you haven't done any macramé before, begin with the Macramé Knots section on pages 6–9 to learn a variety of simple knots, then put them into practice by moving onto the projects. Each project has difficulty rating so you can start with the easier ideas, then build up to creating the more complicated designs. Some of the projects also use crochet techniques, and these are explained on pages 12–15. You will find a macramé board is a very handy surface on which to create your designs. Made from thick foam, you can pin threads to it, there are notches on all sides to hold threads in place, and a grid to keep your patterns evenly spaced. If you are using a synthetic cord that frays easily, try sealing the ends with a lighter—it will melt the fibers together to stop them fraying and can be neater than tying a knot. Hold the lighter an inch or so from the cord end until it melts, but allow to cool before touching the end or putting it down as it could burn your work surface.

The rest of the book has been divided up into four sections—Cute and Colorful, Natural and Homespun, Glitzy and Glamorous, Chic and Contemporary—each of which has its own set of projects.

Cute and Colorful is jam-packed with fun ideas that are ideal for younger crafters. Make a cheerful Owl Key Ring (see page 33) using a range of traditional knots, which is sure to bring a smile to your face, or try the Japanese technique of kumihimo to weave a Braided Charm (see page 42) for your phone or purse. The Braided Shoelaces (see page 44) will brighten up a pair of sneakers no end—try making them in a variety of colors to match every outfit!

Natural and Homespun takes its inspiration from the 1970s; the rustic color palette and natural materials hark back to the simple life. Knot a funky Striped Macramé Shopper (see page 60) from hemp string—perfect for a trip to the local farmers' market—keep the sun from your eyes with a Braided Ribbon Straw Hat (see page 68), or dress up a simple tee with the Tassel Necklace (see page 52), which is a great festival look.

Glitzy and Glamorous brings a bit of sparkle to the mix! The simple Sequin Headband (see page 108) would look great at a wedding or party, and you can practice your micro macramé technique with the Beaded Wave Bracelet (see page 94). The Circular Earrings (see page 105) are also great—they are one of my favorites!

Chic and Contemporary has some really modern ideas. The Chunky Ribbon Necklace (see page 130) is really striking, especially when made in bright colors. For something even more unusual, take a look at the Barbed Wire Elastic Bracelet (see page 138). And no woman can resist a gorgeous purse, so try making the Flower and Nut Clutch Bag (see page 118).

Once you have worked through a few projects you will get the hang of how the knotting works, and you'll quickly realize just how satisfying macramé can be. I hope you enjoy making these projects as much as I have enjoyed designing them!

Macramé knots

Although it's tempting to get started on the projects straight away, it's worth taking a few minutes to practice the knots you will need. Neater knots will create better finished items, so do your homework first!

Backward knot

1 Holding the left-hand filler cord tight, wrap the right-hand working cord around it. Pull the end through the loop created. Pull the cord to tighten the knot.

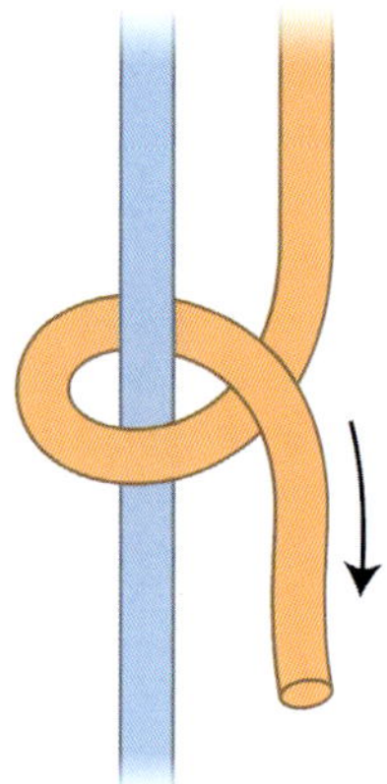

2 Repeat to create a double knot on the left cord.

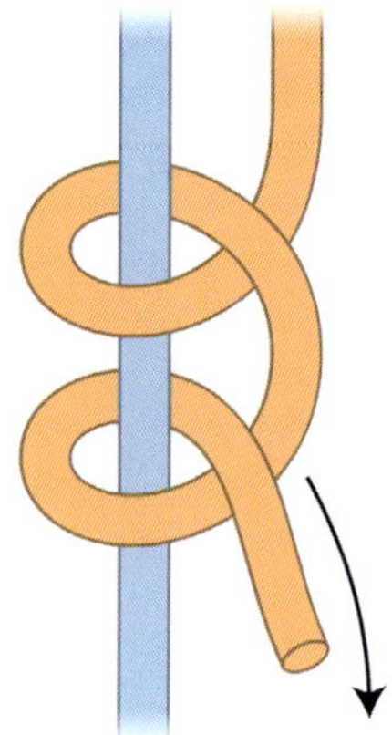

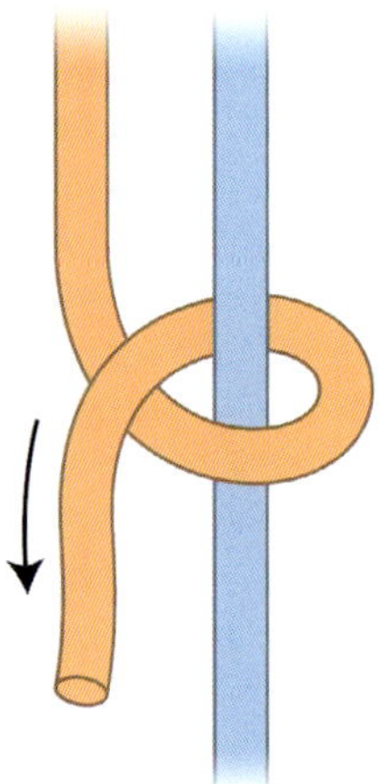

Forward knot

1 Holding the right-hand filler cord tight, wrap the left-hand working cord around it. Pull the end through the loop created. Pull the cord to tighten the knot.

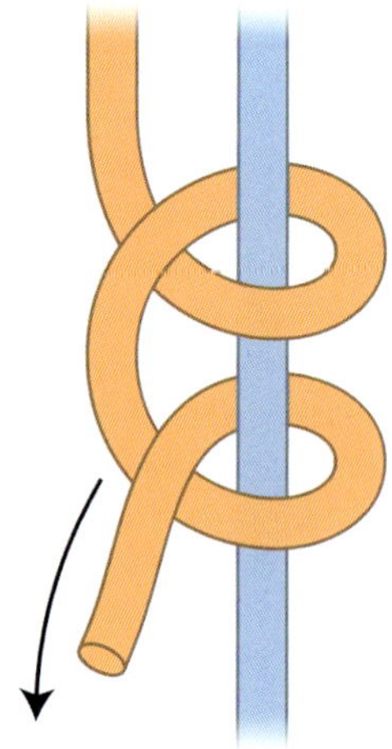

2 Repeat to create a double knot on the right cord.

Josephine knot

1 Take two pieces of cord and create a loop with one of them. Place the second cord underneath the loop. Wrap the second cord end over the first tail of the loop and then under the second tail of the loop.

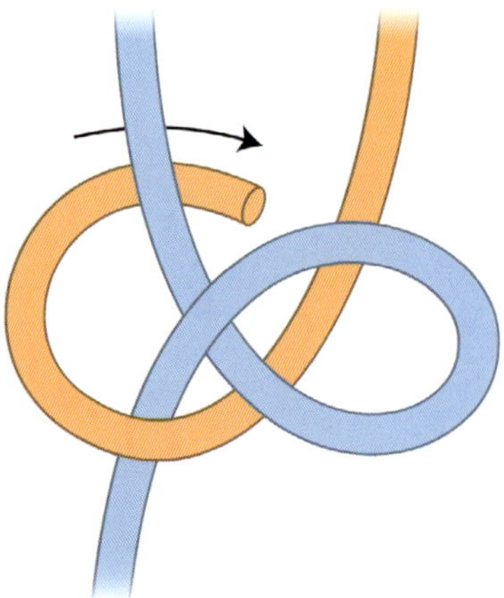

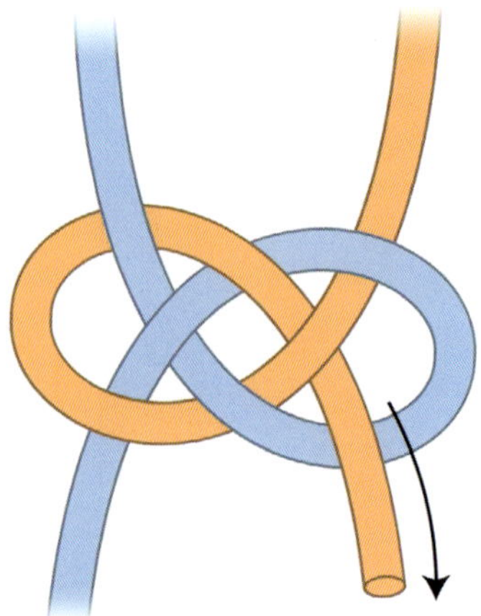

2 Finally, wrap it over the loop and underneath itself to complete the knot.

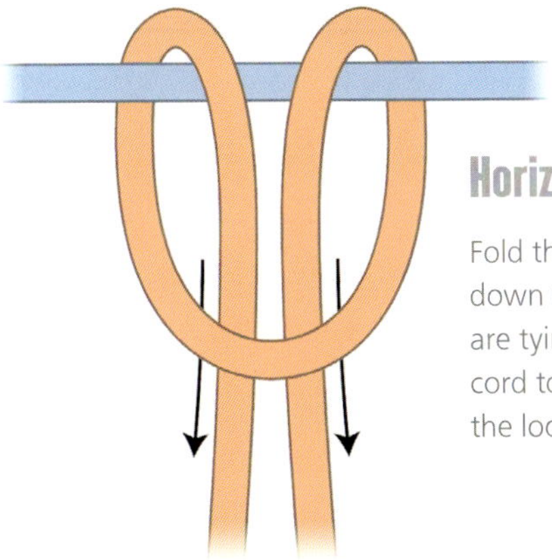

Horizontal lark's head knot

Fold the working cord in half and thread the loop down under the horizontal filler cord, or item you are tying to. Take the two ends over the horizontal cord to the front and thread them down through the loop. Pull to tighten the loop.

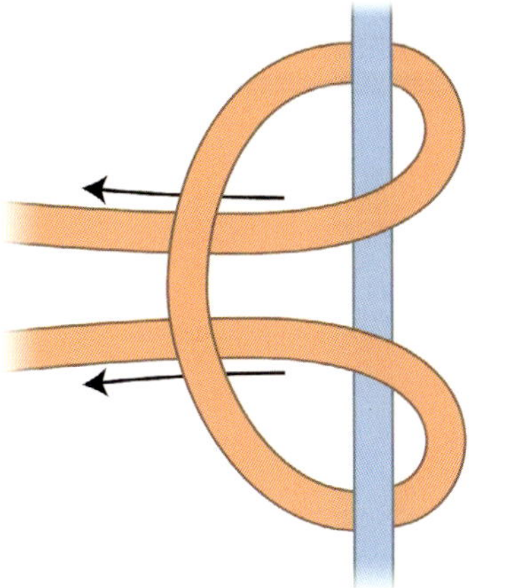

Left vertical lark's head knot

Use the left cord as the working cord and the right cord as your filler cord. Fold the working cord in half and thread the loop under the vertical filler cord from right to left. Take the two ends over the filler cord to the front and thread them through the loop. Pull to tighten the loop.

Right vertical lark's head knot

Use the right cord as the working cord and the left cord as your filler cord. Fold the working cord in half and thread the loop under the vertical filler cord from left to right. Take the two ends over the filler cord to the front and thread them through the loop. Pull to tighten the loop.

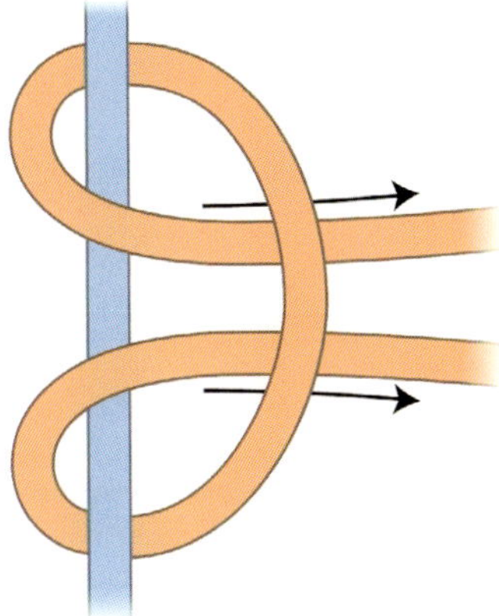

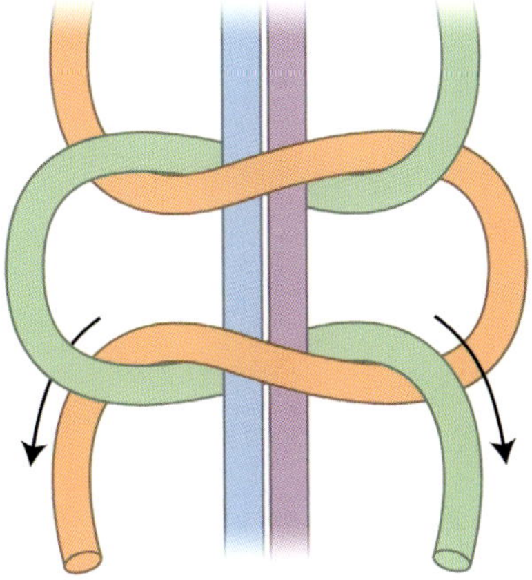

Left facing square knot

The filler cord in the center can be one cord or two, but you need a working cord on either side. Bring the left working cord over the filler cord and under the right cord. Then bring the right working cord under the filler cord and through the loop of the left cord. Repeat in reverse so that the right working cord goes over the filler cord and the left goes under. Pull the knots to tighten.

Right facing square knot

This is the same knot worked in reverse. Bring the right working cord over the filler cord and under the left cord. Then bring the left working cord under the filler cord and through the loop of the right cord. Repeat in reverse so that the left working cord goes over the filler cord and the right goes under. Pull the knots to tighten.

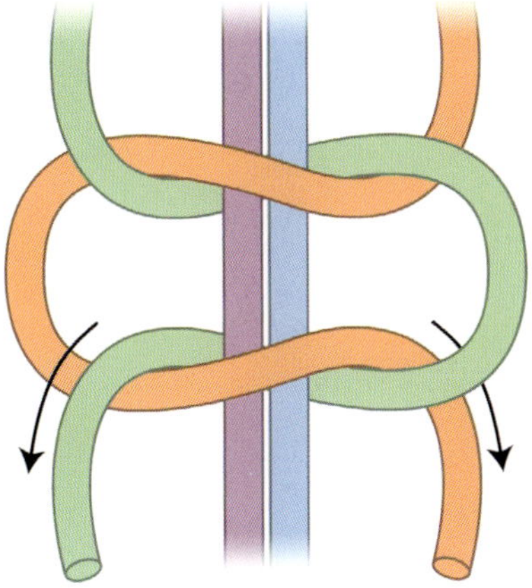

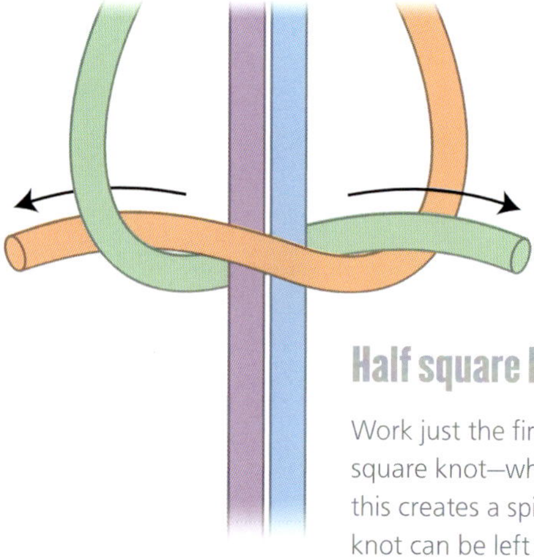

Half square knot

Work just the first half of the square knot—when repeated this creates a spiral effect. This knot can be left facing or right facing depending on which way you want the ridge of the spiral to turn.

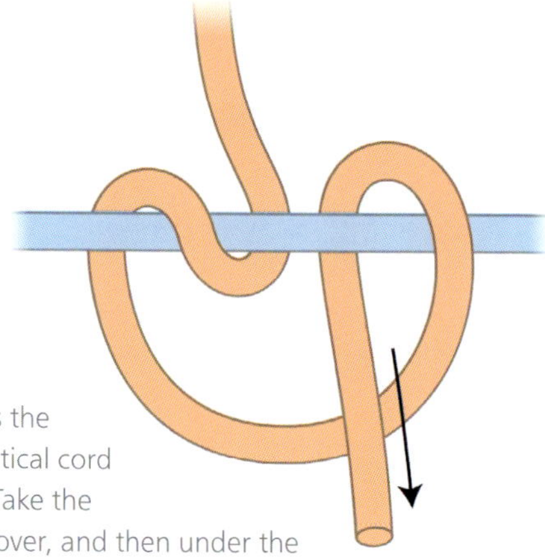

Clove hitch knot

The horizontal cord is the filler cord and the vertical cord is the working cord. Take the working cord under, over, and then under the filler cord, working to the left. Then take the working cord round to the right and over the filler cord to the back, then down through the loop created below the horizontal filler cord. Pull to tighten the knot.

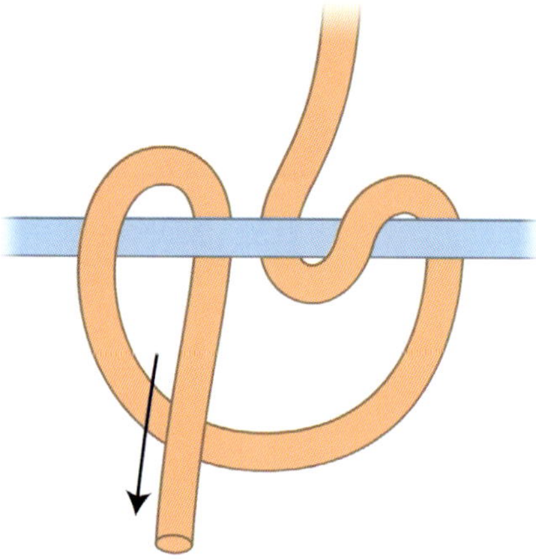

Reverse clove hitch knot

This is the same knot worked in the opposite direction. Take the working cord under, over and then under the filler cord, working to the right. Then take the working cord round to the left and over the filler cord to the back, then down through the loop created below the horizontal filler cord. Pull to tighten the knot.

Vertical clove hitch knot

The vertical cord is the filler cord and the horizontal cord is the working cord. Take the working cord under, over and then under the filler cord, working upward. Then take the working cord round to the right and down, over the filler cord and to the back, then up through the loop created to the right of the filler cord. Pull to tighten the knot.

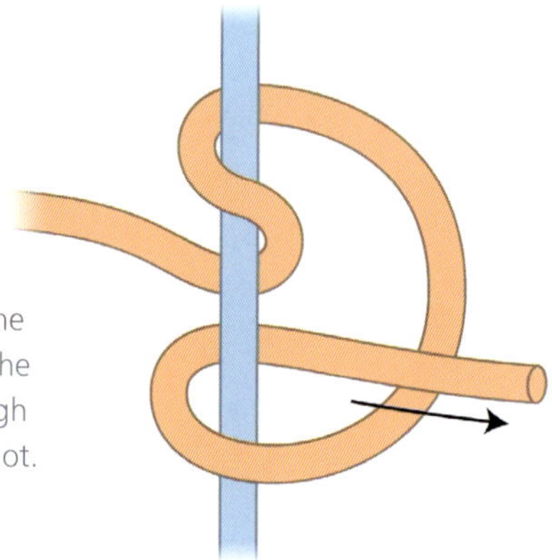

Sliding knot

Hold the cords next to each other, with the ends pointing in opposite directions. Fold the working cord back on itself and loop the end around both cords. Now loop it around twice more and thread the end through the original loop. Pull tight until the knot is tight but can still move up and down the other cord.

Zeppelin bend knot

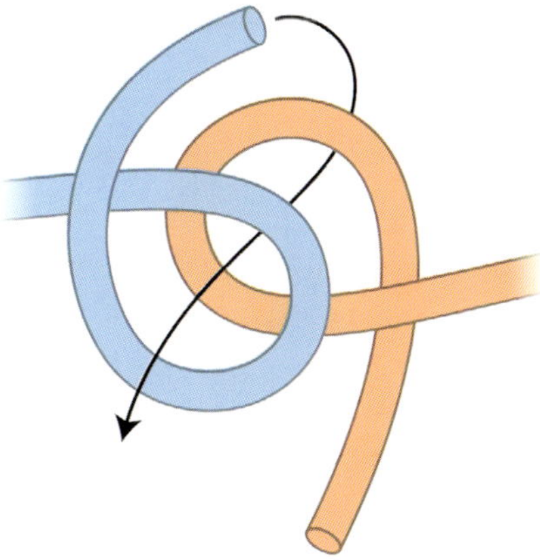

1 Make a clockwise loop with one cord, place on the left, and arrange the upper end toward the top left. Make a counterclockwise loop with the second cord, place on the right, and arrange with the lower end toward the bottom right. Position the first loop on top of the second loop as shown.

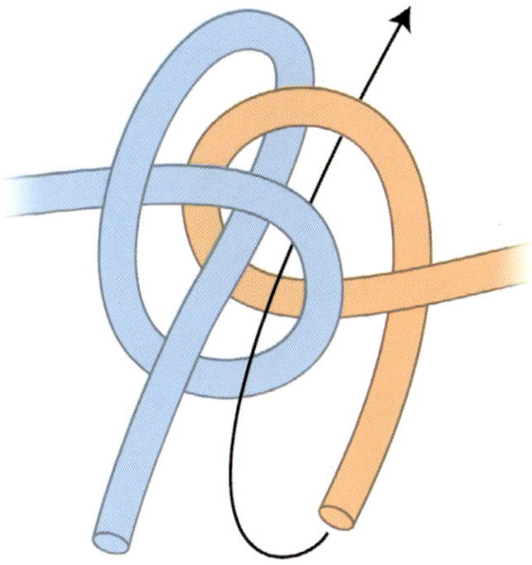

2 Carefully move the left loop on top of the right loop. To complete the left overhand knot, bring the upper end down clockwise, passing it up through both loops. To complete the right overhand knot, bring the lower end upward clockwise, passing it down through the loops.

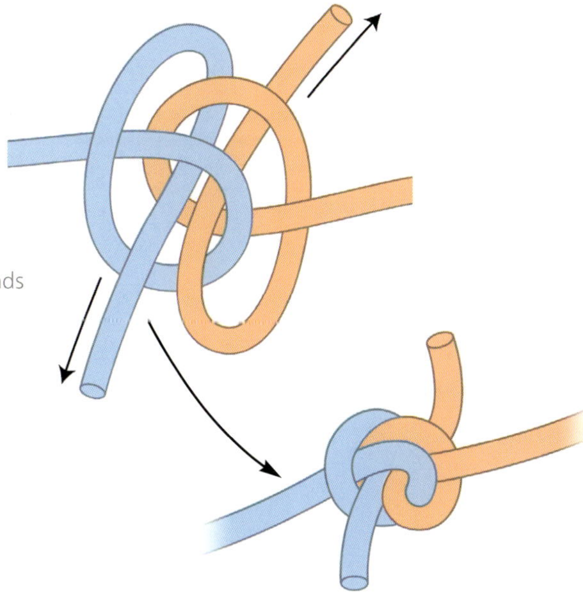

3 Pull on the working ends to tighten the knot.

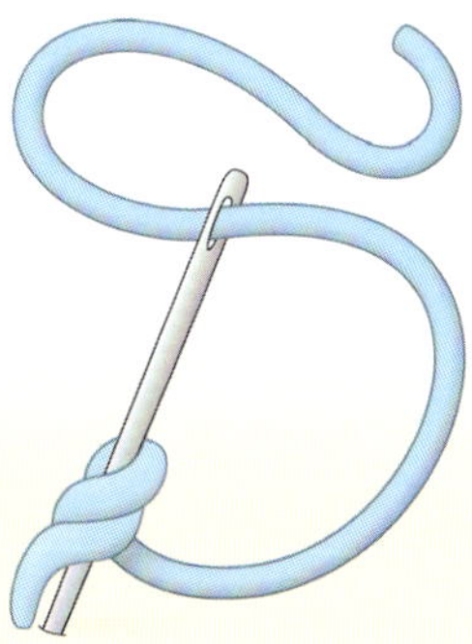

French knot

This sewing technique is used to decorate some projects. Bring the needle up from the back of the fabric to the front. Wrap the thread two or three times around the tip of the needle, then reinsert the needle at the point where it first emerged, holding the wrapped threads with the thumbnail of your non-stitching hand, and pull the needle all the way through. The wraps will form a knot on the surface of the fabric.

Crochet techniques

Chain stitches

Chains are the basis of all crochet. This is the stitch you have to practice first because you need to make a length of chains to be able to make the first row or round of any other stitch. Practicing these will also give you the chance to get used to holding the hook and the yarn correctly.

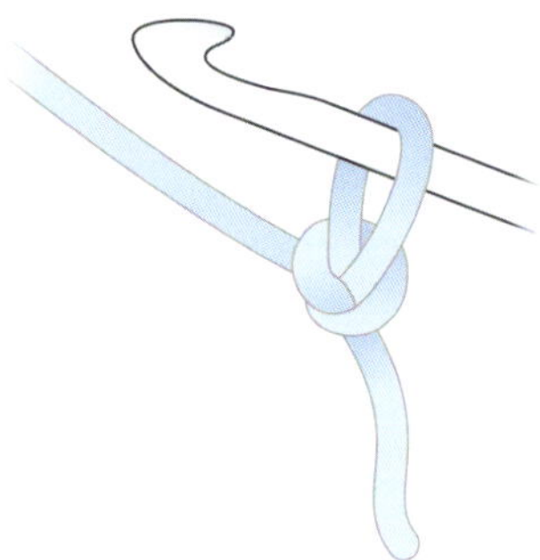

1 Start with the tip of the hook pointed upward, with the slip knot on your hook sitting loosely so there is enough gap to pull a strand of yarn through the loop on the hook.

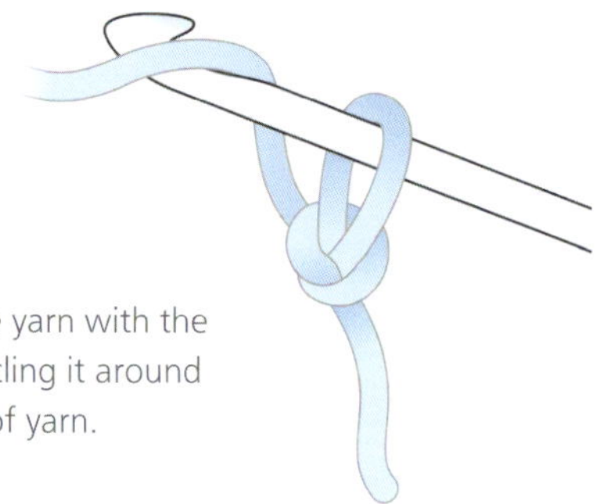

2 Catch the yarn with the hook, circling it around the strand of yarn.

3 As you catch the yarn, turn the tip of the hook downward, holding the knot immediately under the loop on the hook with your left hand between finger and thumb.

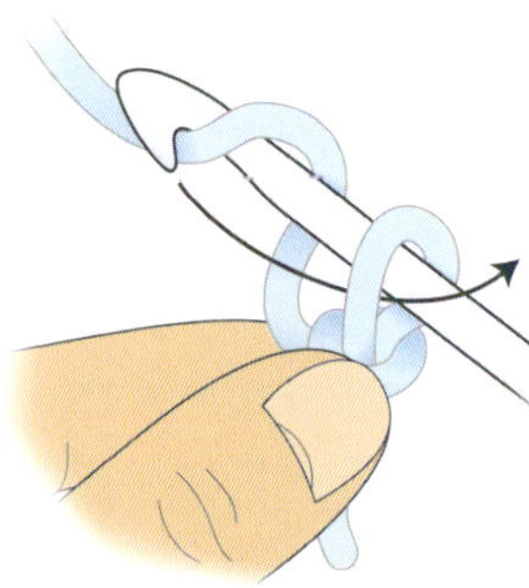

4 Then gently pull the strand of yarn through the loop on the hook. As soon as the tip of the hook comes through the loop, turn the tip of the hook upward.

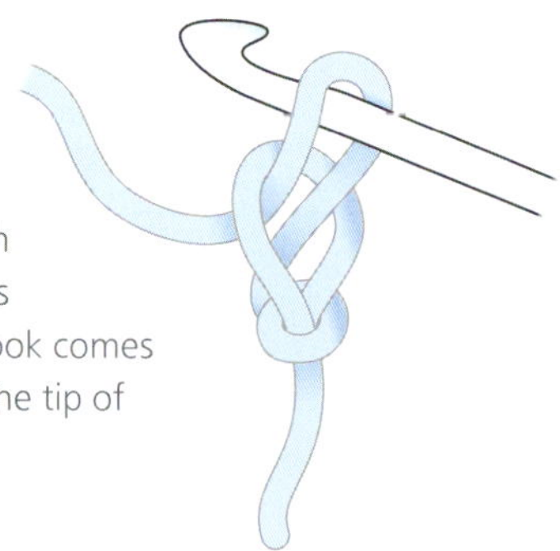

Slip stitch

A slip stitch is the shortest crochet stitch and is usually worked into other stitches rather than into a foundation chain, because it is rarely used to make a whole piece of crochet. It is mainly used to join rounds, or to take the yarn neatly along the tops of stitches to get to a certain point without having to fasten off.

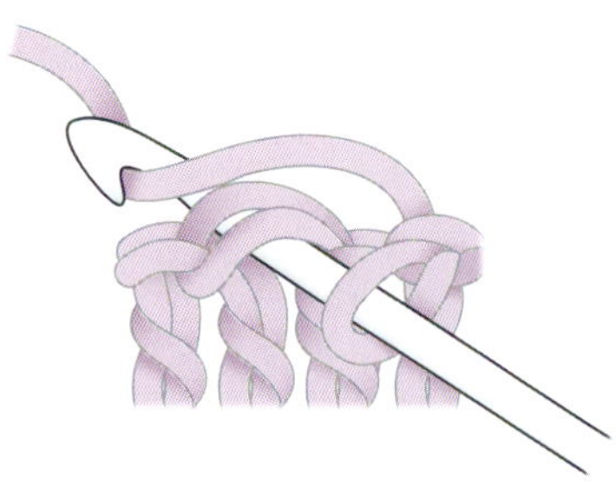

1 To make a slip stitch, first insert the hook through the stitch (chain or chain space). Then wrap the yarn round the hook.

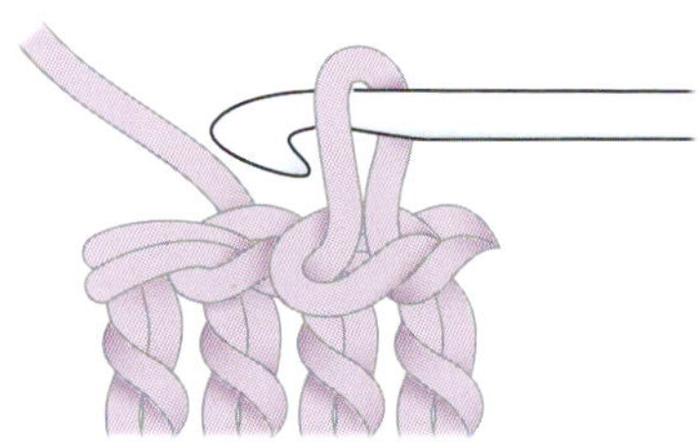

2 Pull the yarn through both the stitch (chain or chain space) and the loop on the hook at the same time, so you will be left with one loop on the hook.

Single crochet (UK double crochet)

Single crochet is the most commonly used stitch of all. It makes a firm, tight crochet fabric. If you are just starting out, it is the best stitch to begin with because it is the easiest to make.

1 Make a foundation chain, then insert the tip of the hook into the second chain from the hook and catch the yarn with the hook by taking the hook around the back of the yarn strand (as shown by the arrow). Pull the yarn through the chain only, with the hook pointed downward. As soon as you have brought the yarn through, immediately turn the hook upward—this will help to keep the loop on the hook and prevent it from sliding off. Keep the hook in a horizontal position all the time.

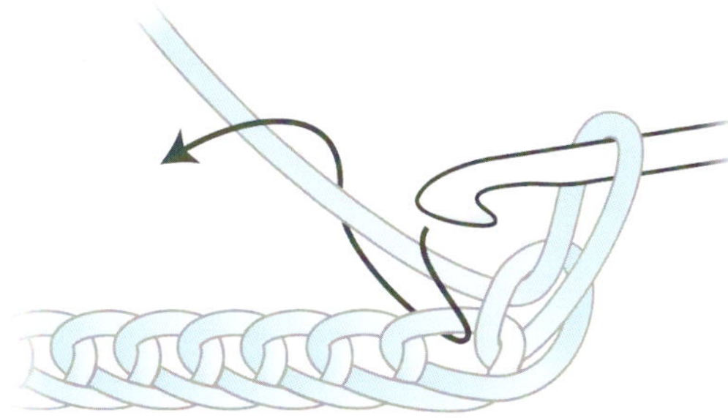

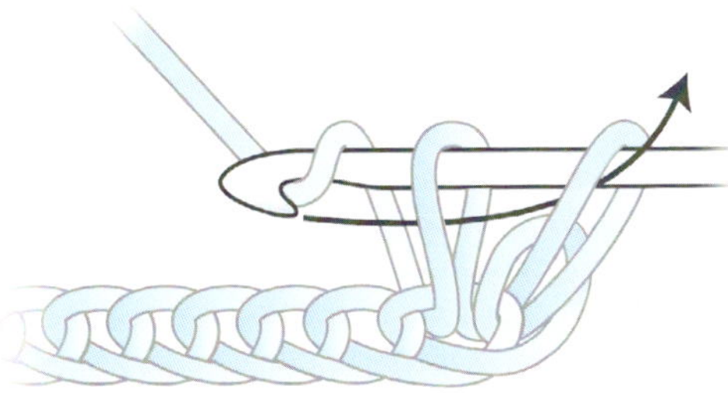

2 You will now have two loops on the hook. Wrap the yarn over the hook again (with the hook sitting at the front of the yarn), turn the hook to face downward, and pull the yarn through the two loops, turning the hook to point upward as soon as you have pulled the yarn through.

3 One loop is now left on the hook. Keep the hook pointed upward (this is the default position of the hook until you start the next stitch). Continue working one single crochet into each chain to the end of the foundation chain.

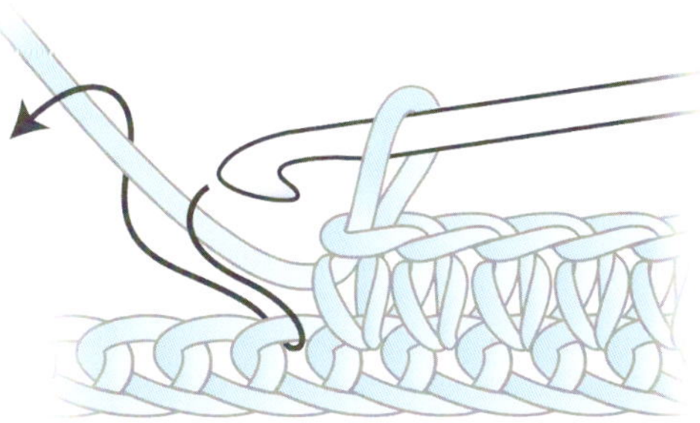

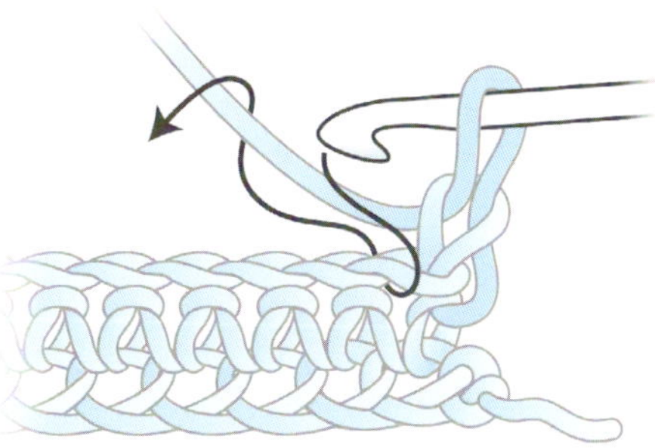

4 Then turn the work to begin the next row. Make one chain and work the first single crochet into the top of the first single crochet in the row below (picking up the two loops at the top of the stitch). Work one single crochet into each single crochet stitch in the row below, to the end of the row. For all subsequent rows, repeat this step.

Half double crochet (UK half treble)

Half double crochet makes stitches that are the next height up from a single crochet stitch. The yarn is wrapped over the hook first before going into the stitch (or space), and then, once pulled through the stitch (or space), there will be three loops on the hook. The middle loop is from the strand that was wrapped over the hook. Before you attempt to pull the yarn through all three stitches, make sure the loops sit straight and loosely on the hook so that you can pull another strand through to complete the stitch.

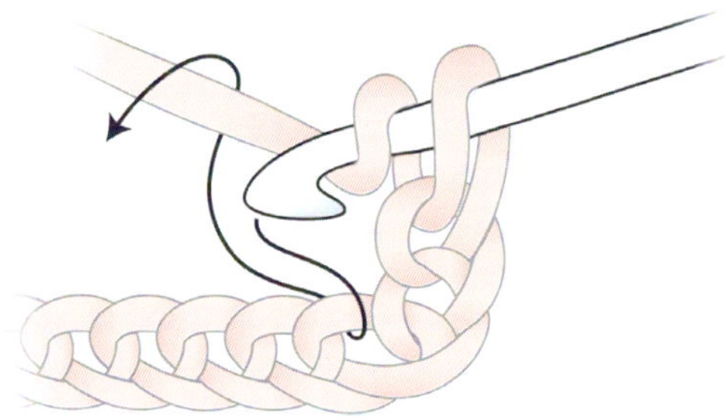

1 Make your foundation chain as usual to start. Before inserting the hook into the work, wrap the yarn over the hook. Then with the yarn over the hook, insert the hook through the third chain from the hook (as shown by the arrow). Work "yarn over hook" again.

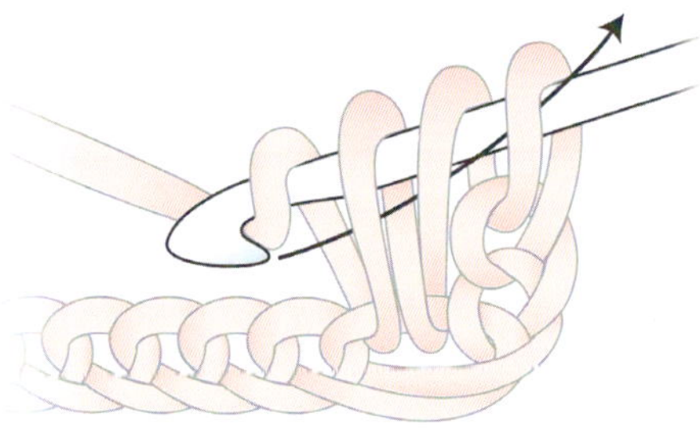

2 Pull the yarn through the chain. You now have three loops on the hook. Yarn over hook again and pull it through all three loops on the hook.

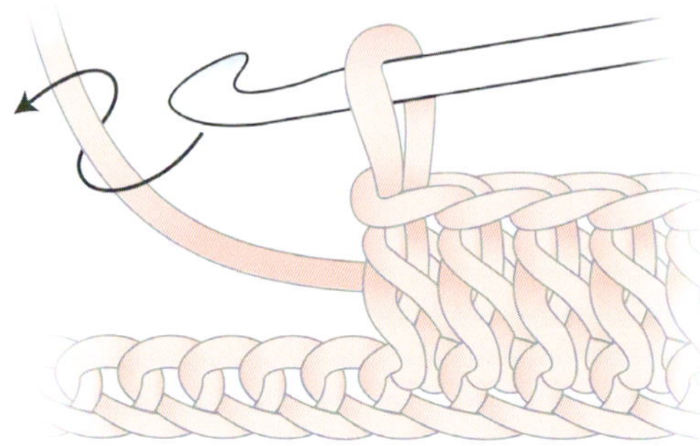

3 You will be left with one loop on the hook. Continue working one half double into each chain to the end of the foundation chain.

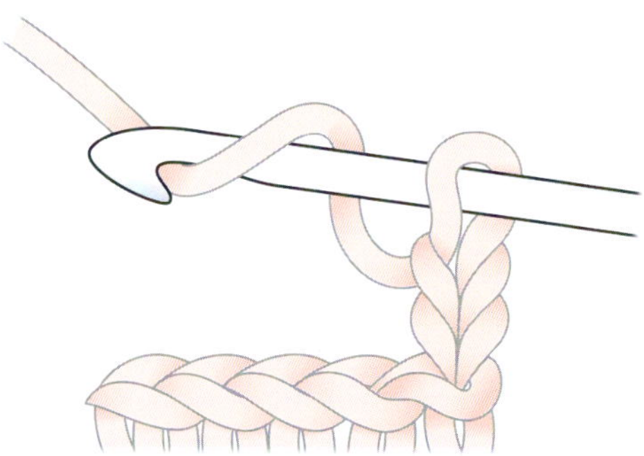

4 Then turn the work to begin the next row. Make two chains. Work one half double into each half double stitch in the row below to the end of the row. For all subsequent rows, repeat this step.

Double crochet (UK treble)

A double crochet is a very common stitch; it gives a more open fabric than a single crochet or a half double—which both give a denser fabric—and the stitches are one step taller than a half double. As with the half double, the yarn is wrapped over the hook first before going into the stitch (or space), and then, once pulled through the stitch, there are three loops on the hook. The middle loop is from the strand that was wrapped over the hook. Before you attempt to pull the yarn through the next two stitches on the hook, make sure the loops sit straight and loosely on the hook so that you can pull another strand through.

1 Before inserting the hook into the work, wrap the yarn over the hook. Then with the yarn wrapped over the hook, insert the hook through the fourth chain from the hook and work "yarn over hook" again (as shown by the arrow).

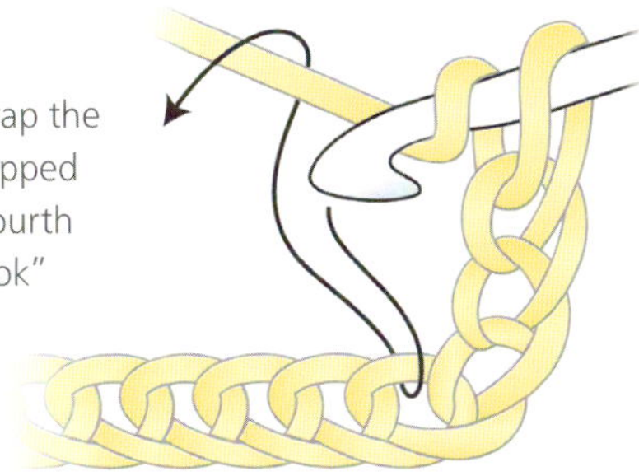

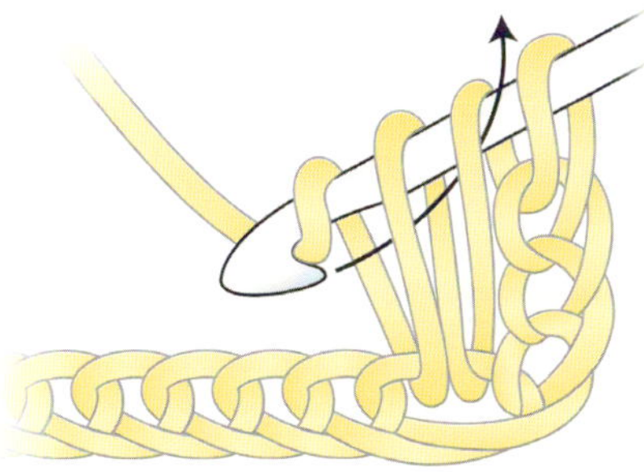

2 Pull the yarn through the chain. You now have three loops on the hook. Yarn over hook again and pull it through the first two loops on the hook.

3 You now have two loops on the hook. Yarn over hook again and pull it through the two remaining loops.

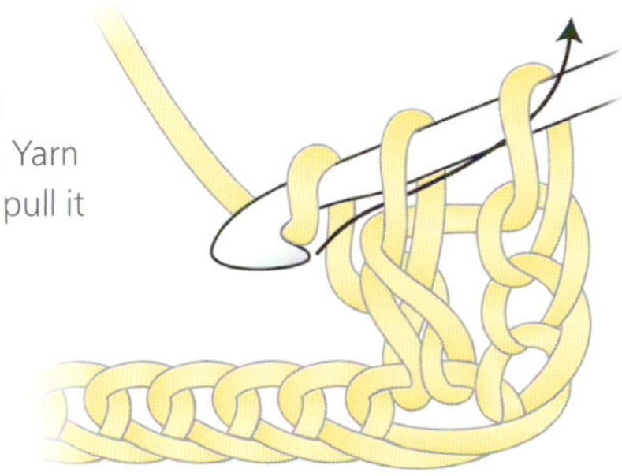

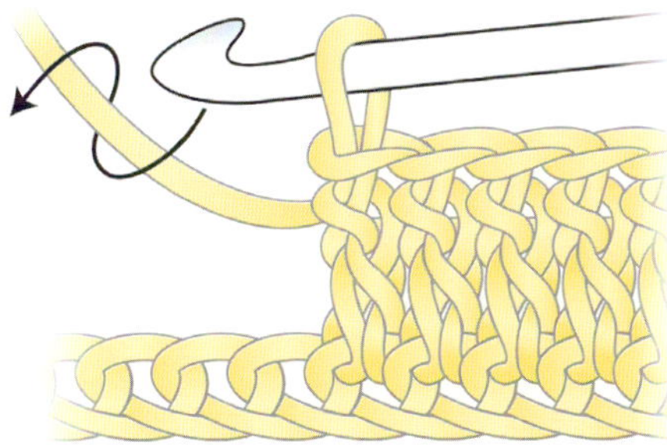

4 You now have one loop on the hook. Continue working one double crochet into each chain to the end of the foundation chain.

5 Then turn the work to begin the next row. Make three chains. Work one double crochet into each double stitch in the row below to the end of the row. For all subsequent rows, repeat this step.

CHAPTER 1:

CUTE AND COLORFUL

Buddhist treasure mesh cuffs

An ideal way to practice your basic knotting technique before going onto some of the more difficult projects. These bracelets are delicate and pretty, too.

You will need

Orange bracelet

- 6in. (15cm) length of cord
- Macramé board and pins
- Sixteen 72in. (180cm) lengths of peach 0.5mm nylon cord
- Scissors
- Lighter
- Two 1⅜in. (3.5cm) ribbon crimps
- Pliers
- 9 jump rings
- Lobster claw clasp

Green and mustard bracelet

- 6in. (15cm) length of cord
- Macramé board and pins
- Three 72in. (180cm) lengths of green 0.5mm nylon cord
- Three 72in. (180cm) lengths of mustard 0.5mm nylon cord
- Two 1⅜in. (3.5cm) ribbon crimps
- Pliers
- 9 jump rings
- Lobster claw clasp

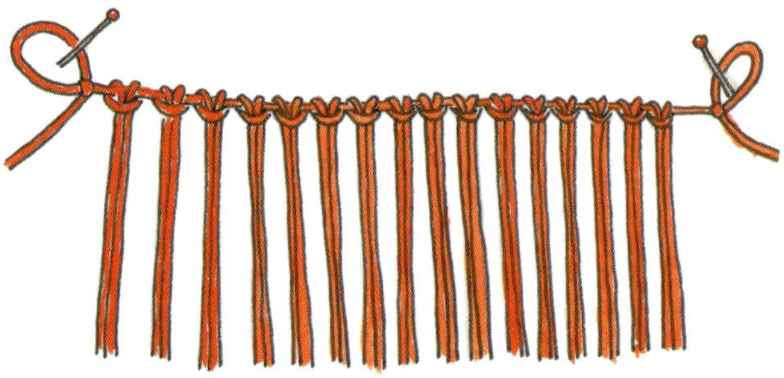

Peach bracelet

1 Tie a knot at each end of the 6in. (15cm) length of cord for the anchor. Pin this to your macramé board. Fold the 16 long threads in half and attach each to the anchor cord using lark's head knots.

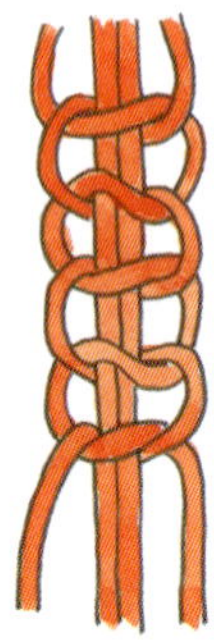

2 Take the first four cords of the row and work two left facing square knots (see page 7). Pull them tight to create a solid knot. Repeat all along the row.

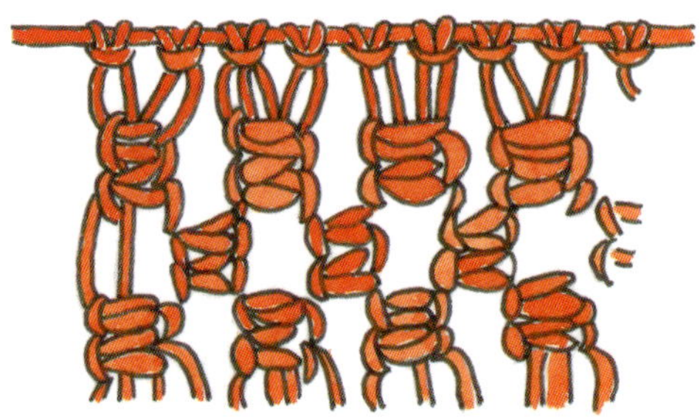

3 For the next row, skip the first two cords and then work two left facing square knots with each set of four cords. There will be two cords left loose at each end. Repeat steps 2 and 3 until your piece measures approx. 6in. (15cm).

4 Tie pairs of cords together with a tight knot, trim, and melt with a lighter to seal the end.

5 Place a ribbon crimp over the end of the piece and shut with a pair of pliers. Repeat on the other end, trimming the anchor cord to the same width as the bracelet and knotting the ends before adding the ribbon crimp.

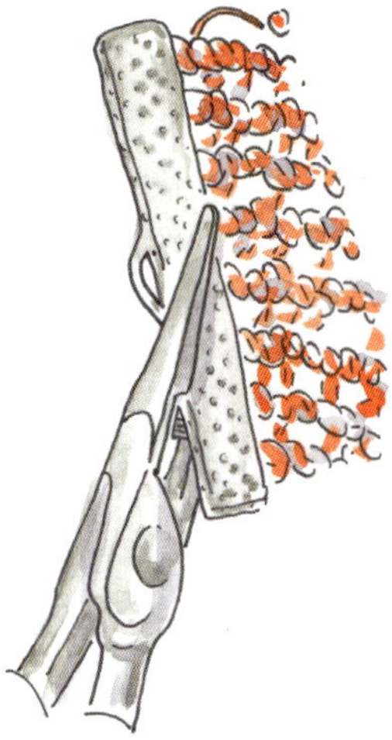

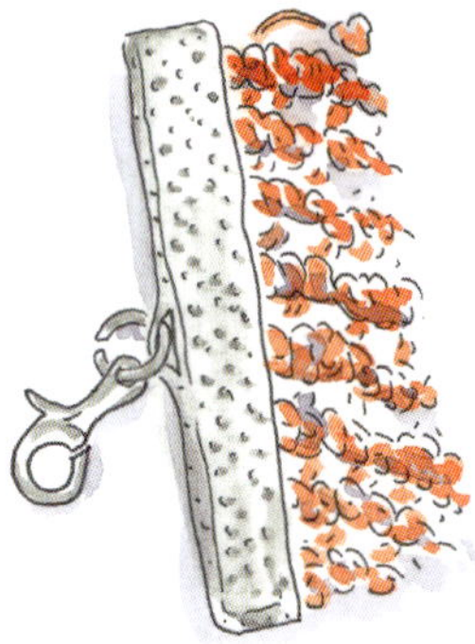

6 Use a jump ring to add the lobster claw clasp to one end of the bracelet.

7 Add eight jump rings to the other end of the bracelet.

Green and mustard bracelet

1 Make an anchor cord as before and add the cords, alternating the colors.

2 Work one and a half left facing square knots with each bunch of four cords along the row.

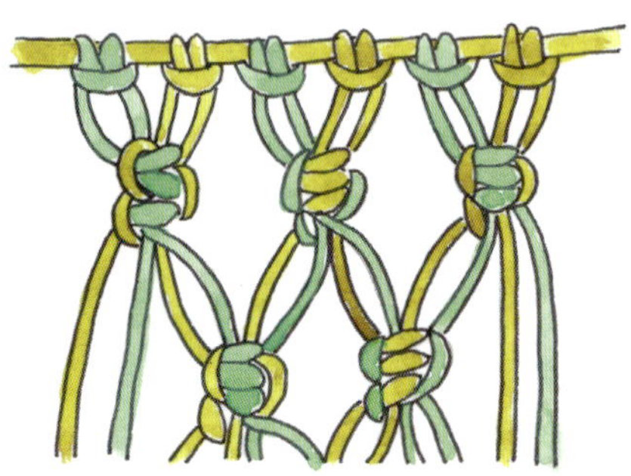

3 Leave a gap of ¼in. (5mm) between each row of knots to create the open effect shown. On the second row, skip two cords before tying another one and a half square knots. Repeat again; there will be two cords left on the end.

4 Repeat steps 2 and 3 until the piece measures 6in. (15cm), then finish as for the peach bracelet.

T-shirt yarn necklace

T-shirt yarn is made using excess fabric from the fashion industry. Combine it with some bright feathers and use simple knots to make a statement boho necklace that will look brilliant at a festival this summer!

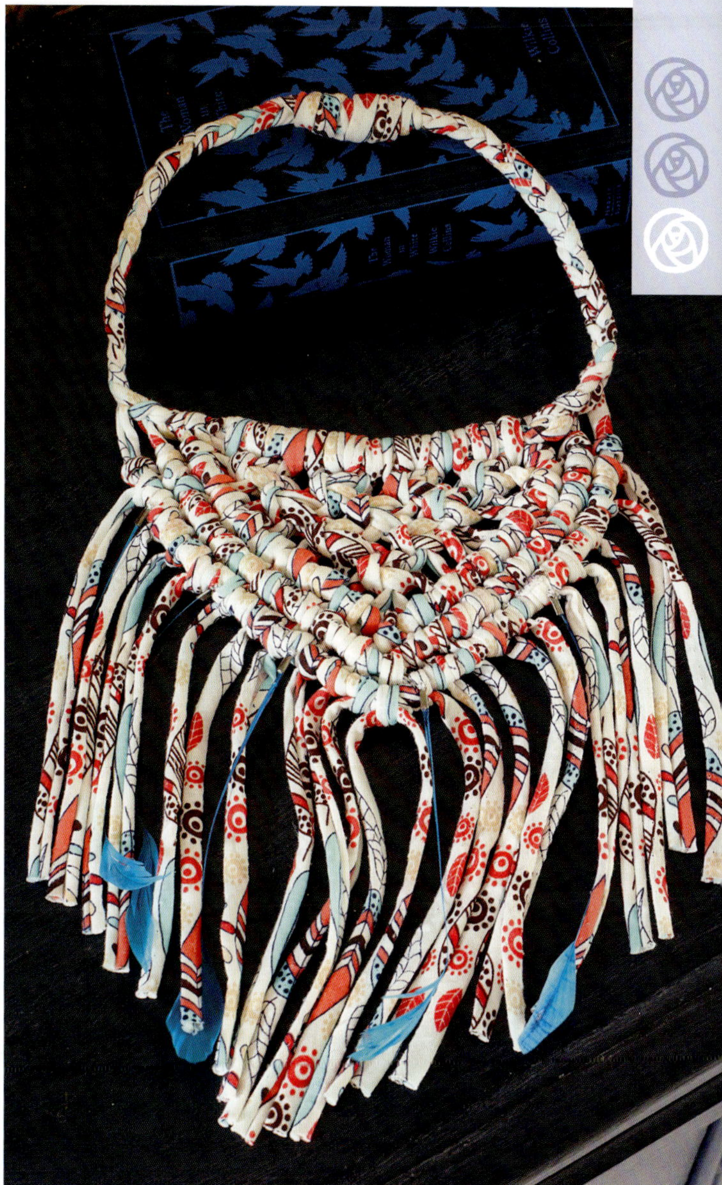

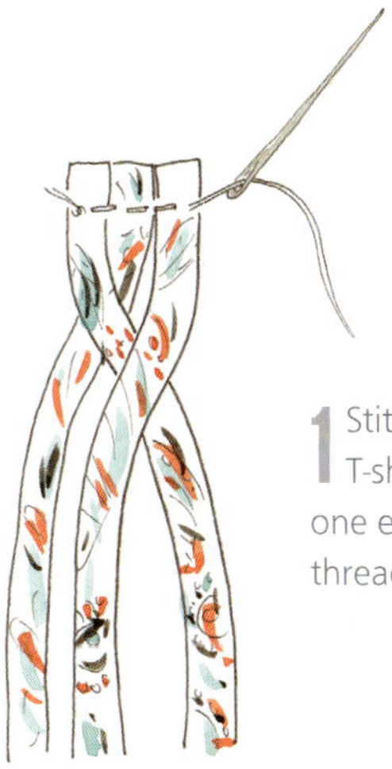

1 Stitch the three pieces of T-shirt yarn together across one end using a needle and thread, and then plait.

2 Pin the central section of the plait to your macramé board. Fold each of the 60in. (150cm) tassel pieces in half and tie all eight of them along the plait using lark's head knots (see page 7).

You will need

- Three 48in. (120cm) lengths of T-shirt yarn
- Sewing thread and needle
- Macramé board and pins
- Eight 60in. (150cm) lengths of T-shirt yarn
- Six 20in. (50cm) lengths of T-shirt yarn
- Scissors
- 5 turquoise feathers
- 5 crimp cord ends, ⅛ x ⅜in. (4 x 9mm)
- Pliers
- Short length of T-shirt yarn

3 Divide the threads into groups of four and work a square knot (see page 7) with each group to create the first row of the necklace.

4 To form the triangle shape of the necklace, on the second row, skip the first two threads, then work three square knots. There will be two threads remaining on the right side.

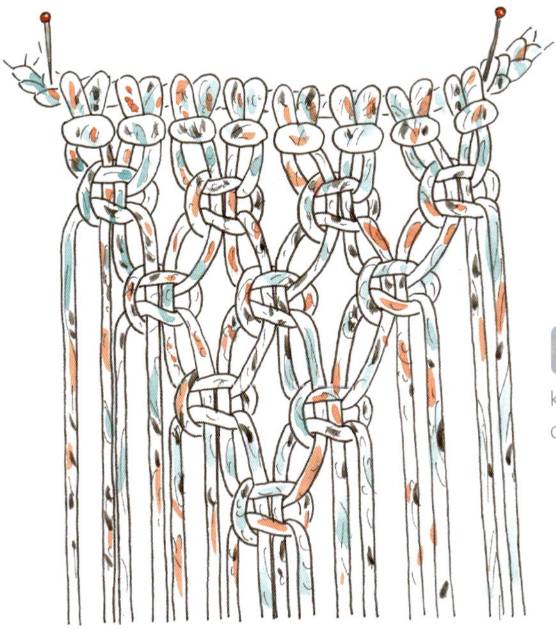

5 On the third row, skip the first four threads, then work two square knots. There will be four threads remaining on the right side.

6 On the final row, skip the first six threads, then work one left square knot. There will be six threads remaining on the right side.

7 Take one of the 20in. (50cm) filler cords and pin to the board just to the left side of the necklace. Tie eight clove hitch knots (see page 8) to this using the ends of the tassel cords, working from the top to the center. Repeat on the right side with a second 20in. (50cm) filler cord and then knot the two filler cords together in the center with two forward knots.

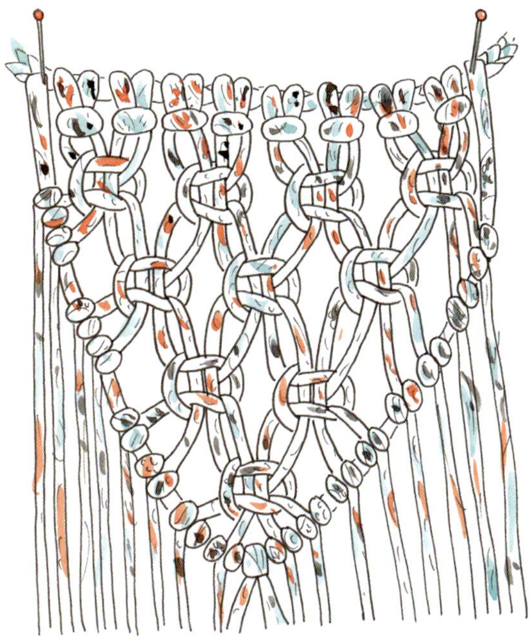

8 Repeat two more times with the other four 20in. (50cm) filler cords. Trim the tassel ends to 6in. (15cm). Sew the top ends of the filler cords into the back of the necklace.

9 Trim the feathers to 6in. (15cm). Place a crimp cord end over the end of each feather and close with the pliers.

10 Sew the ring at the top of each cord end to the necklace so the feathers sit among the tassels.

11 To close the necklace, sew the two ends together and hide the join by wrapping a short length of yarn around it and threading the ends into the wrapped section to neaten.

Josephine knot belt

Create a stunning belt from the fabrics of your choice to emphasize your waist and give your outfit a unique look. Once you have made the fabric tubes, the actual knot is really simple.

You will need

- Four 1¼ x 40in. (3 x 100cm) strips of floral fabric
- Two 1¼ x 40in. (3 x 100cm) strips of pink metallic jersey fabric
- Sewing thread and needle
- Six 40in. (100cm) lengths of 5mm piping cord
- Scissors
- Sewing machine
- Four 2 x 4¾in. (5 x 12cm) rectangles of felt
- Four 2¾ x 5½in. (7 x 14cm) rectangles of floral fabric
- 6 metal snaps

1 Fold each strip of fabric in half, right sides together, and sew along the long side with a ¼in. (5mm) seam allowance. Turn right side out.

2 Sew a piece of thread to the end of one of the pieces of cord and then pull it through one of the fabric tubes. Repeat with the other five lengths of cord and fabric tubes.

3 Take one of the metallic pink cords (A) and position as shown.

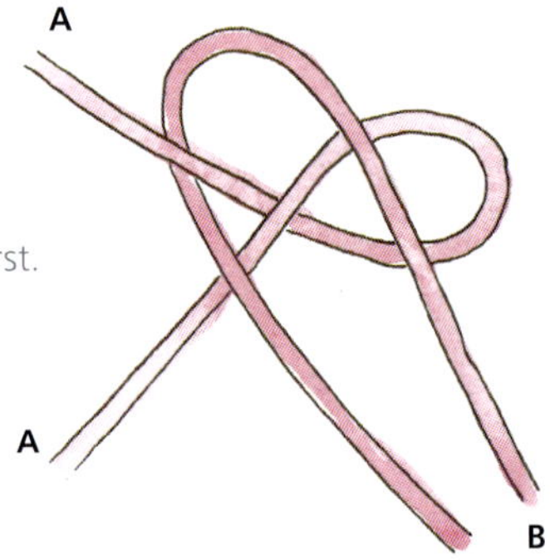

4 Using the diagram as a guide, thread the second metallic pink cord (B) through the first.

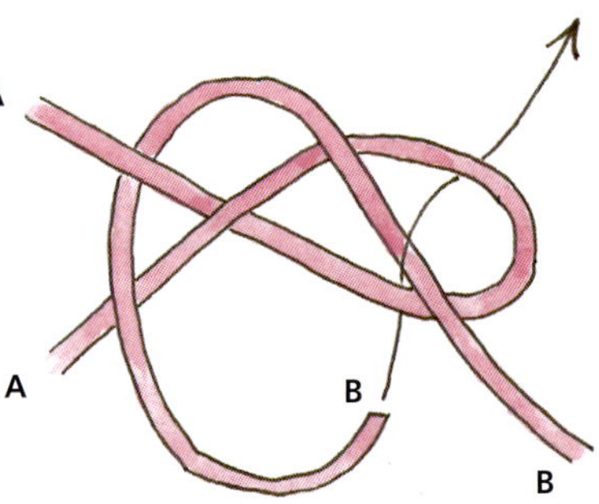

5 Bring the bottom right-hand cord under, over, and then under, as shown by the arrow.

6 This makes an interlaced knot. Even the loops up.

7 Using the floral cords, follow the threading pattern of the first cords. Then repeat a final time with the remaining floral fabric cords to complete. Ensure that the metallic cords are between two floral ones.

8 To strengthen the knot, sew the cords together on the back of the knot so it stays in position.

9 Neaten the ends so they are all the same length, and then sew together using the sewing machine.

10 Place each felt rectangle into the center of the wrong side of a fabric rectangle. Fold the fabric over the edge all round and baste in place.

11 Place the cord ends from one side of the knot in between two pieces of fabric, with the fabric felt sides together.

12 Using the sewing machine, sew around the edges of the fabric, then across twice to divide it into three rectangles. Sew diagonally both ways across each rectangle to form a cross.

13 Repeat on the other end of the belt with the other two pieces of fabric. Set two snaps in the top and bottom segment of each rectangular section, following the instructions on the packet.

Fabric braided purse

Use strips of voile fabric to make a pretty purse. You could make it larger to become a clutch bag by adding extra rows of braiding.

You will need

- 20 x 60in. (50 x 150cm) of voile fabric in each of pink, lime green, mushroom, and pale blue
- Scissors
- Macramé board and pins
- Yarn needle
- Needle and thread
- 10in. (25cm) cream zipper
- 10in. (25cm) diameter circle of cream fabric

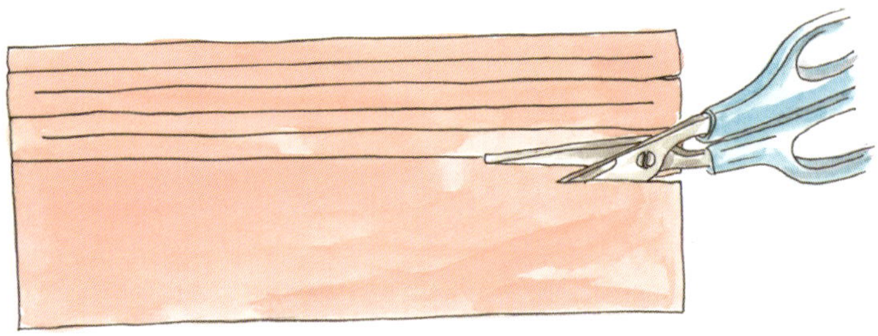

1 Start by cutting the fabric into ⅜in. (1cm) wide strips: working along the long side of the first color fabric from left to right, cut the first strip stopping ⅜in. (1cm) from the right-hand end. Make the next cut from right to left, beginning ⅜in. (1cm) below the previous cut and stopping ⅜in. (1cm) from the left-hand end. Continue cutting in alternate directions down the fabric, stopping ⅜in. (1cm) from the end each time—this way you create a continuous strip so you don't have so many ends to sew into the final purse.

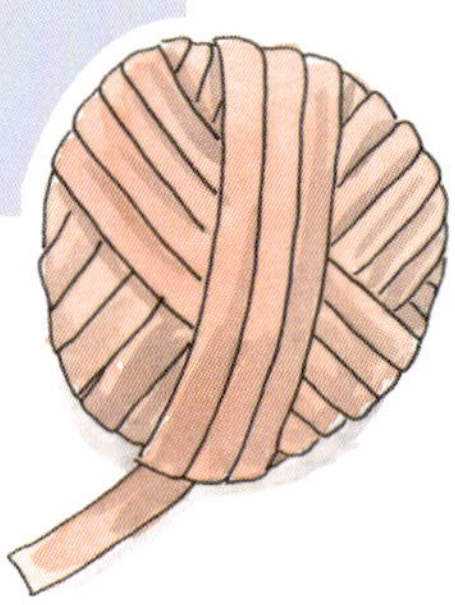

2 Roll the strip into a ball. Repeat with all four colors—these fabric strips will be your cords to make the purse.

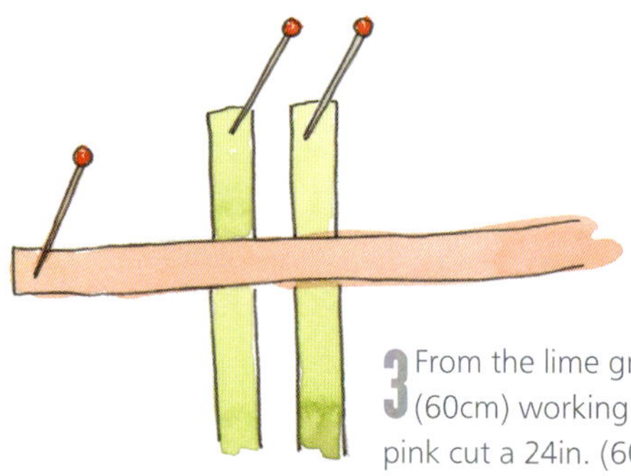

3 From the lime green cut two 24in. (60cm) working cords. From the pink cut a 24in. (60cm) long filler cord. Pin the lime green working cords vertically to the macramé board, and the pink filler cord horizontally over the top.

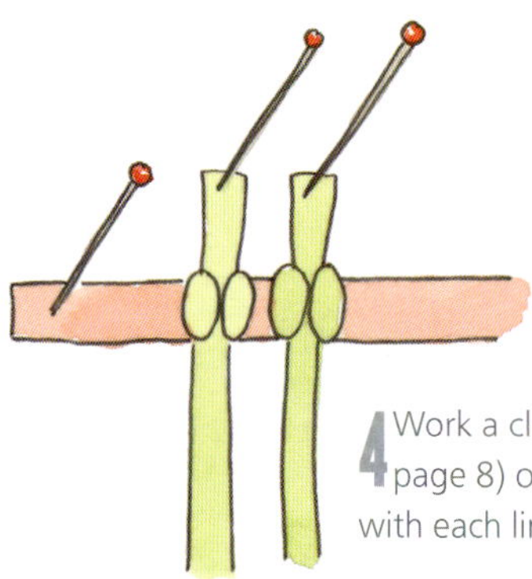

4 Work a clove hitch knot (see page 8) on the pink filler cord with each lime green working cord.

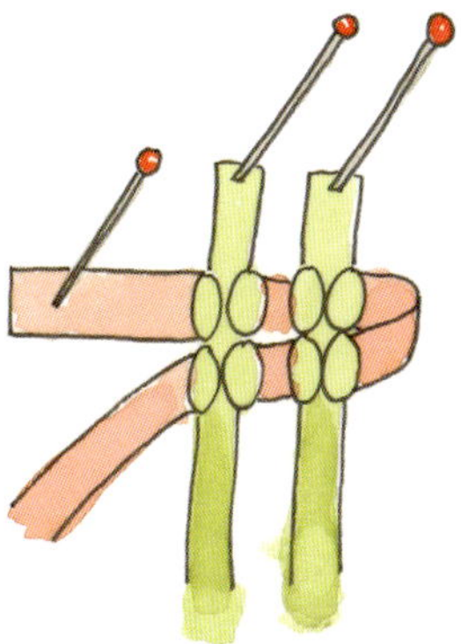

5 Fold the pink filler cord round and back on itself and work two more clove hitch knots on it with the green working cords.

6 From the mushroom cut an 8in. (20cm) cord and wrap it round into a loose circle.

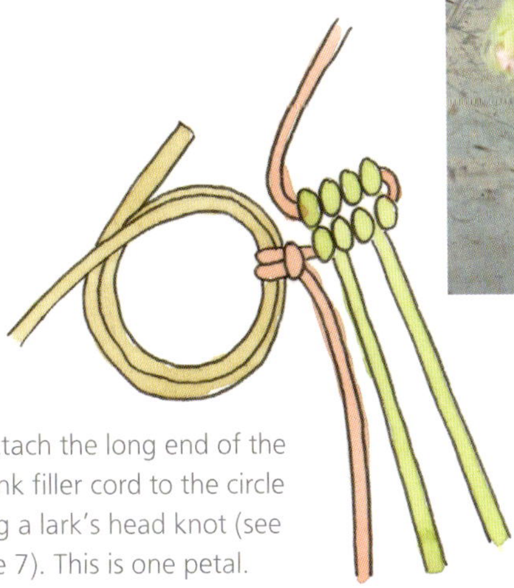

7 Attach the long end of the pink filler cord to the circle using a lark's head knot (see page 7). This is one petal.

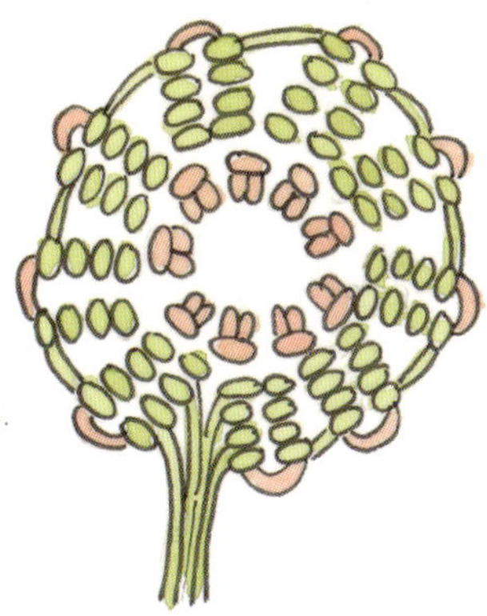

8 Repeat steps 4, 5, and 7 eight more times to complete a circle of nine petals.

9 Pull the ends of the looped center cord to tighten the circle.

10 Turn the piece over and then sew in all the ends.

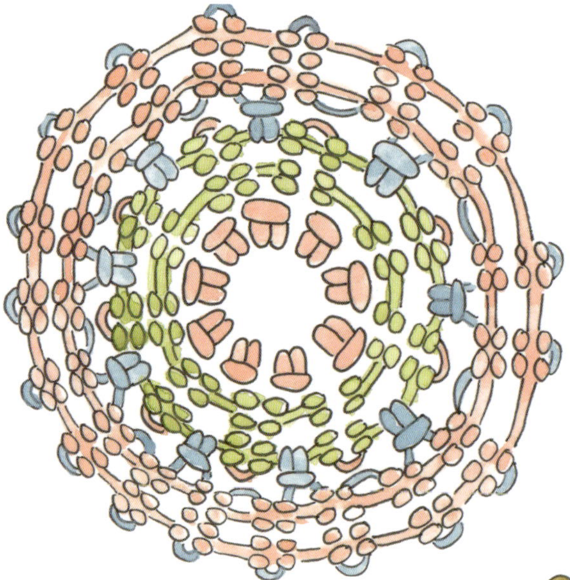

11 For the second round, repeat steps 3–5 but use two 48in. (120cm) pink cords for the working cords and a 32in. (80cm) blue filler cord. Attach the long end of the filler cord between two petals on the outermost working cord of the previous round. Work two petals for each one in the first round, 18 in total, using lark's head knots to attach every other petal to the round below.

12 For the third round, work as step 11 but using three 60in. (150cm) blue working cords and a 40in. (100cm) mushroom filler cord. Since you have three working cords, each petal will be made of two rows of three clove hitch knots. Work three petals each time before joining to the round below.

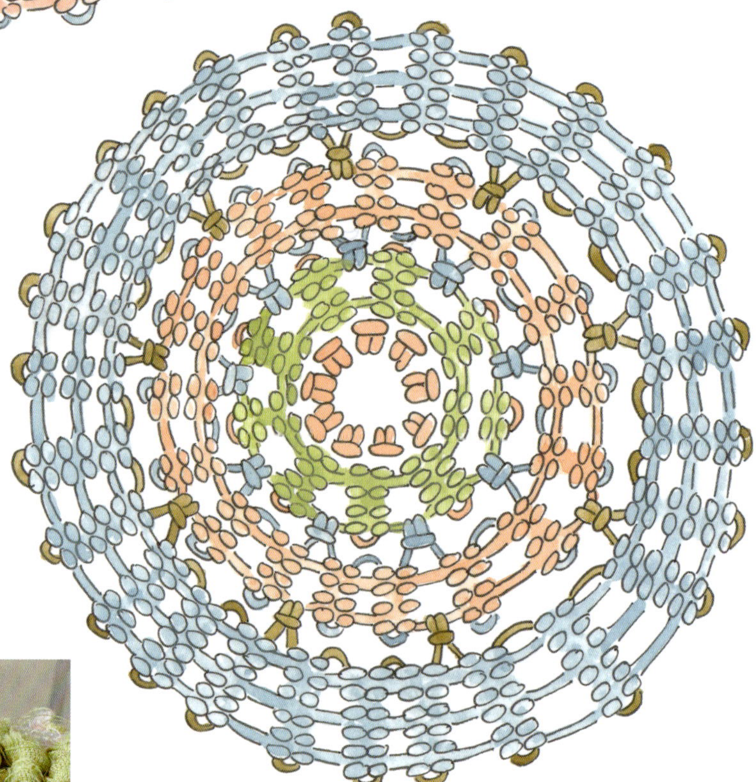

13 For the fourth round, work as step 11 but using four 100in. (250cm) mushroom cords and a 60in. (150cm) lime green filler cord. Since you have four working cords, each petal will be made of two rows of four clove hitch knots. Work four petals each time, before joining to the round below.

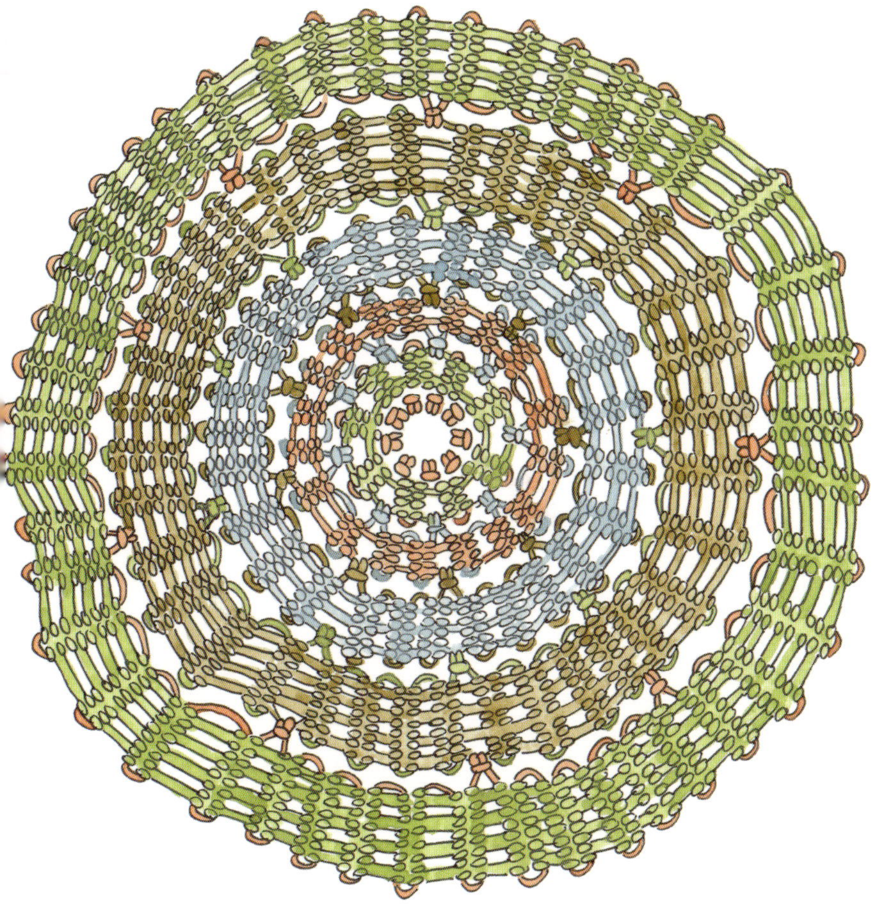

14 For the fifth row, work as above but using five 160in. (350cm) lime green cords and a 100in. (250cm) pink filler cord. Since you have five working cords, each petal will be made of two rows of five clove hitch knots. Work five petals each time before joining to the round below.

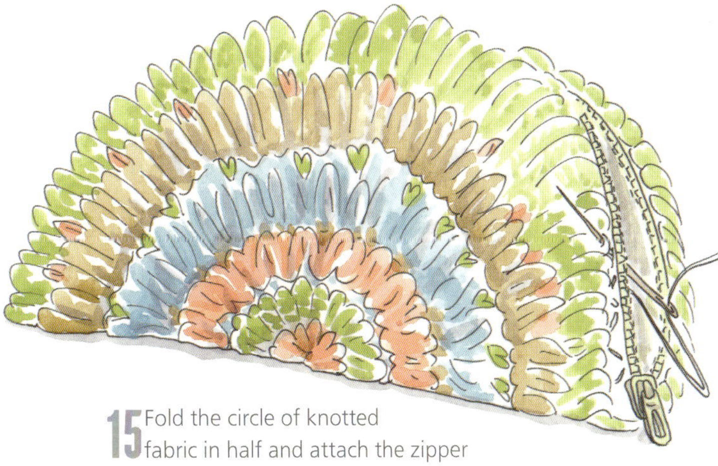

15 Fold the circle of knotted fabric in half and attach the zipper between the curved edges using slipstitch.

16 Open the purse out flat. Fold under all around the edge of the circle of cream fabric and slipstitch it to the inside of the purse to line it.

Globe knot key ring

Use brightly colored satin cords to make a handy globe knot key ring. The trick to keeping the shape is a center of aluminum foil!

You will need

- 60in. (150cm) of turquoise satin cord
- Rolling pin
- 60in. (150cm) of pink satin cord
- 60in. (150cm) of lime green satin cord
- 60in. (150cm) of cream satin cord
- Aluminum foil
- Scissors
- Split ring

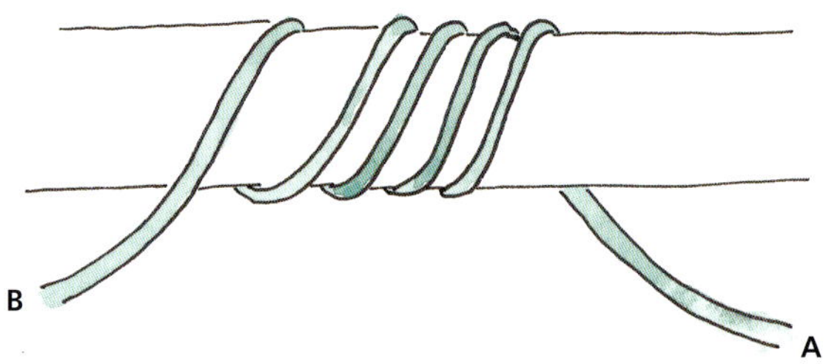

1 Take the turquoise cord and wrap the center of the length around the rolling pin four times. The right-hand end is A and the left-hand end is B, as labeled in the diagram.

2 Take A and work it over, under, over, under the wrapped cord.

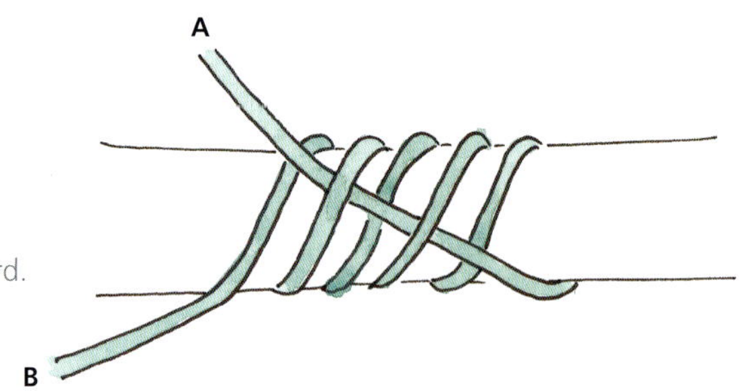

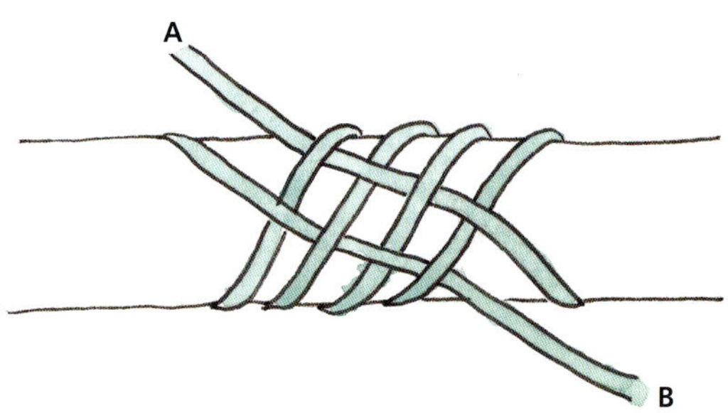

3 Then take B and work it over, under, over, under the wrapped cord.

4 Now bring cord A round and down over cord B, and then work it over, under, over, under, over.

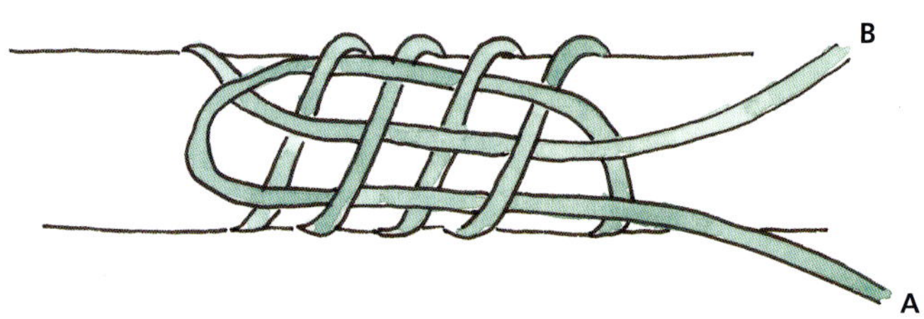

5 Take cord B round and up, and then work it over, under, over, under, over.

6 Then take cord A round and up and work it between the top two cords: over, under, over, under, over, under.

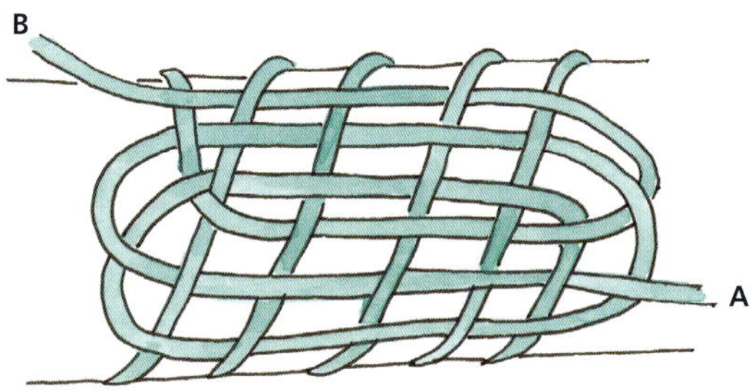

7 Finally take cord A round and down and work it between the bottom two cords: over, under, over, under, over, under, over.

8 Turn the rolling pin over and take cord A under, over, under, over, under in the gap above cord B.

9 Now follow the path you have made with the first cord using each of the other three cords in turn.

10 Carefully slide the knot off your rolling pin. Take a piece of foil, roll it into a ball about 1in. (2.5cm) diameter, and insert it into the knot.

11 Gently tighten your knot around the foil ball.

12 Thread the cord ends through the knot and trim. Poke the last little bit of each end into the ball to hide.

13 Thread the split ring through one set of loops.

Owl key ring

Update the classic macramé owl from the 1970s with brightly colored nylon threads, and then turn it into a handy key ring.

1 Fold each of the cords in half and attach to the split ring using lark's head knots (see page 7).

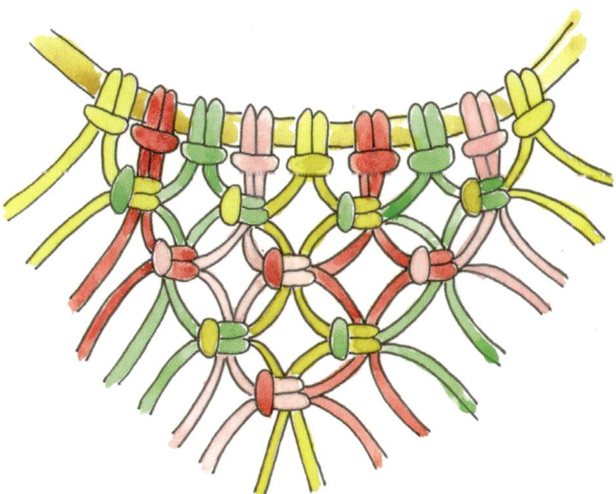

2 Skipping the very first and last cords, work four square knots (see page 7) on the first row. Then skip the first three and the last three cords on the second row and work three square knots. On the third row, skip five cords at each end and work two square knots, and finally on the fourth row work one square knot with the center four cords.

You will need

- Three 60in. (150cm) lengths of 0.1mm mustard nylon cord
- Two 60in. (150cm) lengths of 0.1mm green nylon cord
- Two 60in. (150cm) lengths of 0.1mm dusky pink nylon cord
- Two 60in. (150cm) lengths of 0.1mm bright pink nylon cord
- Split ring
- 2 black glass seed beads
- Scissors
- Lighter

3 Take the left-most cord and work a clove hitch knot (see page 8) on the next cord to the right. Repeat across to make eight clove hitch knots to the center. Repeat on the right side. Work a forward knot (see page 6) with the two central cords. Repeat the whole sequence a second time so you have a double row of knots.

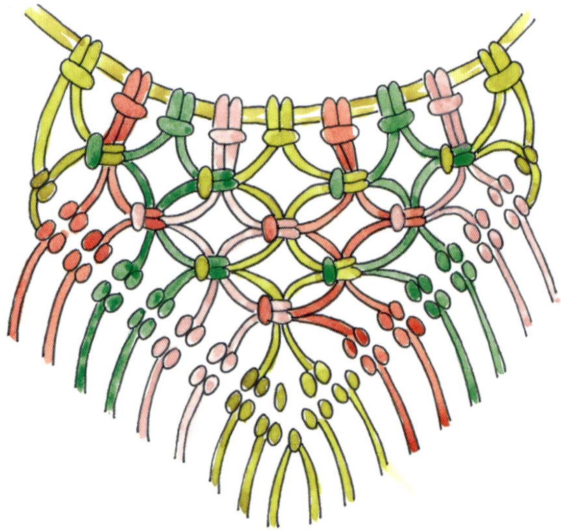

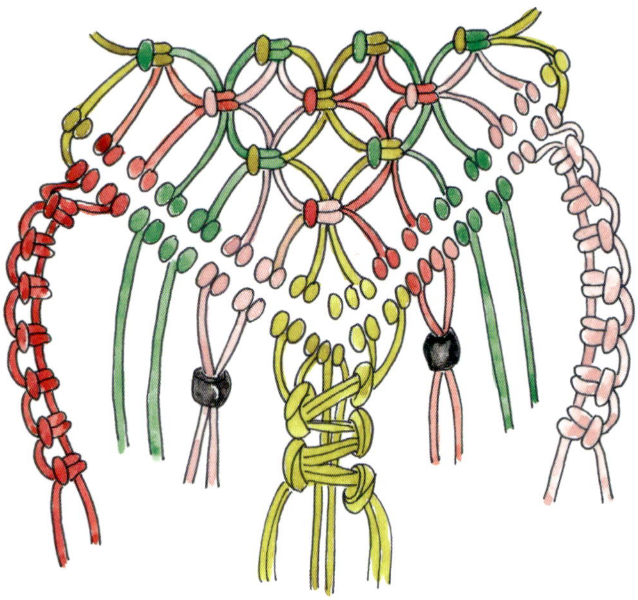

4 Take the central mustard threads and work two square knots; there will be two working cords on either side and two central filler cords. Thread a black bead onto each pair of bright pink threads for the eyes. Using the outer cords, work seven vertical lark's head knots on both sides.

5 Using all the threads, work another two rows of clove hitch knots, working from the outside into the center each time, as in step 3.

6 Using the two outer cords on the left, work a row of 12 vertical lark's head knots. Repeat on the right. Divide the remaining cords in the center into three (there will be five cords in two of the bunches and four in one bunch), then work two square knots with each bunch.

7 Take two of the filler cords and thread from front to back through the top of the knot.

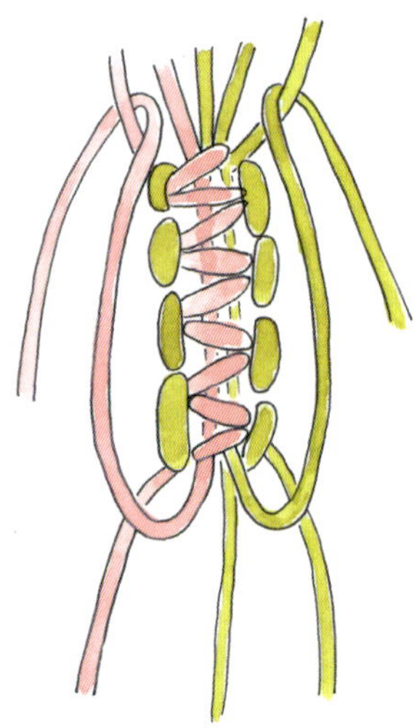

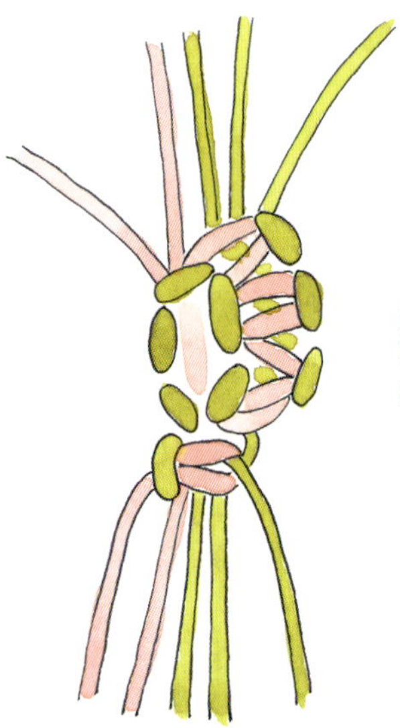

8 Pull tight to curve the square knots into a bump, and then make another square knot beneath to secure.

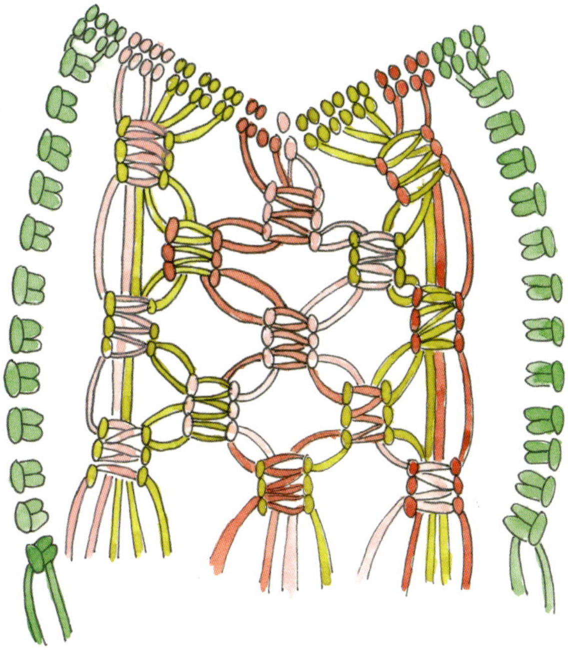

9 Repeat to make a row of three bumps. On the next rows, miss the two outer cords on each side so you make only two bumps. Make another three alternating rows of bumps for the chest and then complete with two rows of normal square knots.

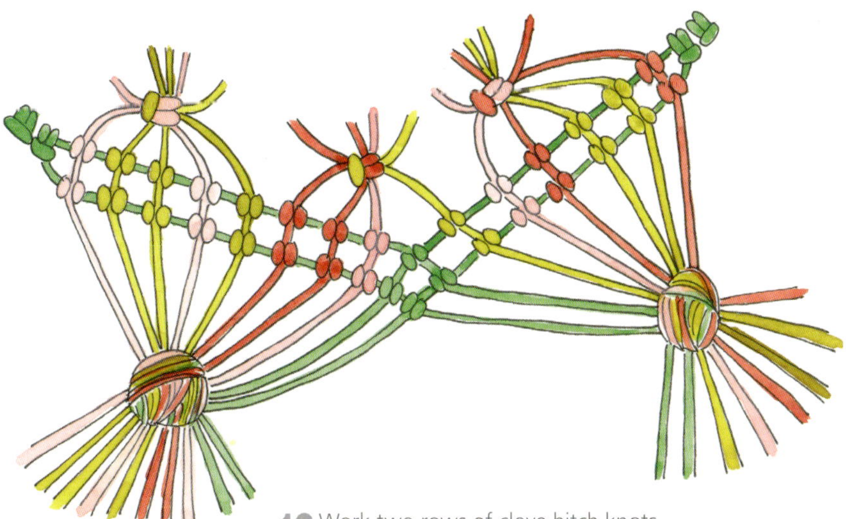

10 Work two rows of clove hitch knots into the center as in steps 3 and 5. Then tie the cords into two equal bunches to make the feet. Trim the ends to an equal length and seal with a lighter.

Monkey fist knot necklace

Use bright and colorful paracords to make monkey fist knot beads, then combine these with leather beads made in the same way to create this simple but effective necklace.

You will need

- Two 60in. (150cm) lengths of pink and orange paracord
- 60in. (150cm) lengths of pink, orange and turquoise paracord
- Four 60in. (150cm) lengths of turquoise leather cord
- 40in. (1m) of orange leather cord
- Scissors
- Thick needle

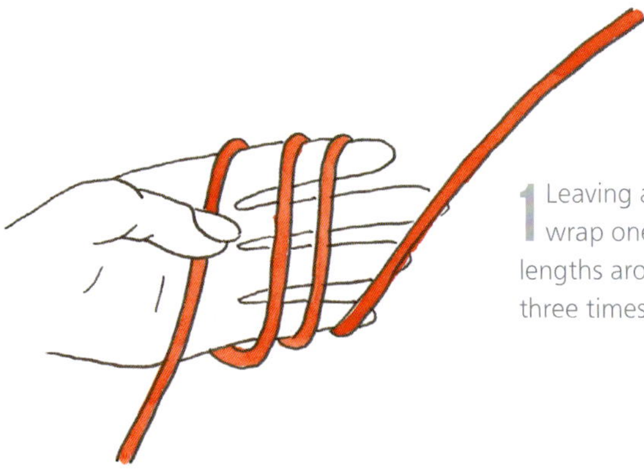

1 Leaving an 8in. (20cm) end, wrap one of the paracord lengths around your hand three times.

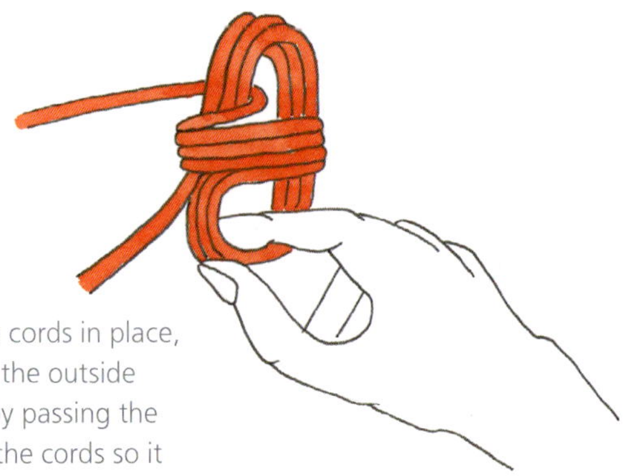

2 While holding the first set of three cords in place, wrap the cord three times around the outside at the middle of the first set. Finish by passing the working cord through the center of the cords so it is in the correct place for the next move.

3 Now wrap the cord three times around the wraps made in step 2, passing through the inside of the knot each time.

4 Working slowly, gradually begin tightening the knot, starting at one end and working your way through the knot. You may need to do this a few times to get it as tight as you require. Thread the ends into the knot and trim to neaten.

5 Repeat with the other two lengths of paracord and then with each of the turquoise leather cords, to make seven beads in total.

6 Thread the beads onto the center of the orange leather cord in the order shown.

7 Referring to the sliding knot instructions on page 8, work two sliding knots with the ends of the leather cord so that you can adjust the size of the necklace and take it on and off easily.

Chevron necklace

This necklace is made up of small sections of chevron braid joined together with short sections of chain. You could make it longer or wider by increasing the number of threads you use, or by braiding extra rows.

You will need

- Fourteen 30in. (75cm) lengths of orange perle cotton thread
- Four 30in. (75cm) lengths of olive green perle cotton thread
- Four 30in. (75cm) lengths of cream perle cotton thread
- Four 30in. (75cm) lengths of brown perle cotton thread
- Four 30in. (75cm) lengths of turquoise perle cotton thread
- Macramé board and pins
- Scissors
- Sewing needle
- Four ⅜in. (1cm) lengths of chain
- 12 jump rings
- Two 6in. (15cm) lengths of chain
- Lobster claw clasp
- Pliers

1 Take two of each color thread, fold in half, and tie a knot in the threads approximately 3in. (7.5cm) from the top.

2 Arrange the threads so the outer threads are orange, the next in are olive green, then cream, then brown, then turquoise. Repeat the pattern with the remaining threads. Pin to the macramé board.

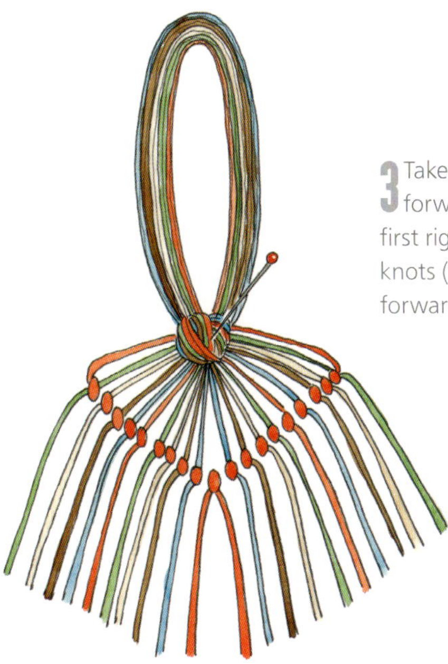

3 Take the first left orange thread and work 9 forward knots (see page 6). Then take the first right orange thread and work 9 backward knots (see page 6). Join the threads using a forward knot.

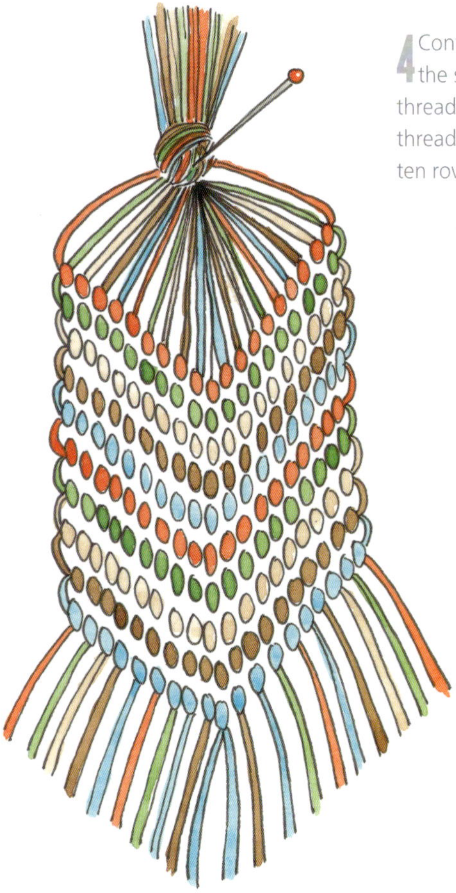

4 Continue making the chevron braid in the same way, always using the outer threads and working inward until each thread has been used once and there are ten rows of braiding.

5 Untie the knot at the top and cut the threads loose. Sew the ends into the back of the chevron section and trim the excess. Put to one side.

6 Repeat steps 1–5 with another ten threads, but arrange the threads so the first two are orange, the next two olive green, then two cream, two brown, and finally two turquoise.

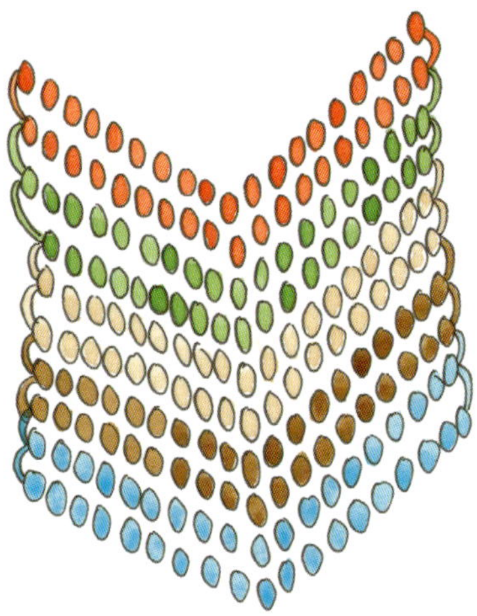

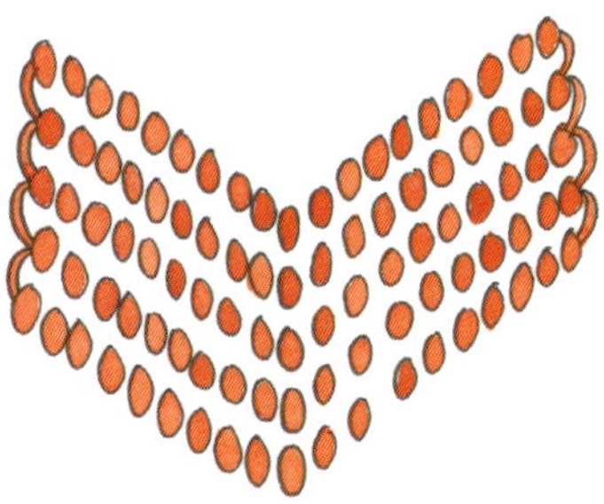

7 For the final section, tie ten orange threads together and work just five rows of braiding, before threading the ends and trimming.

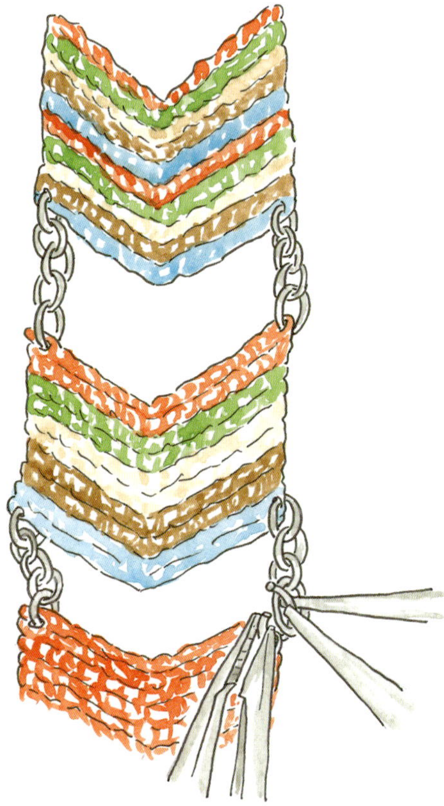

8 Lay out the sections as shown in the diagram and join together using the ⅜in. (1cm) lengths of chain and eight of the jump rings.

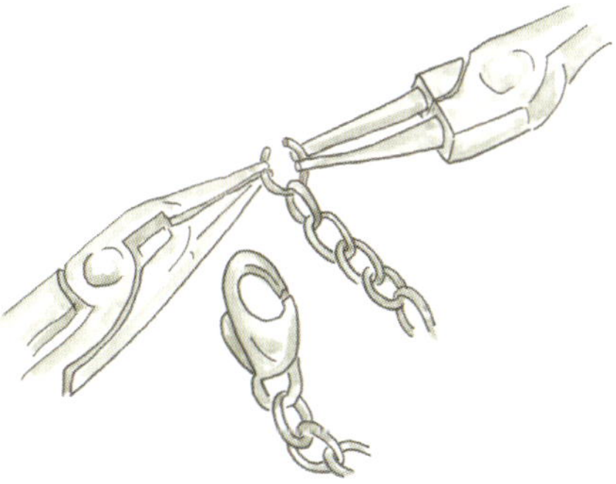

9 Attach the longer chains on either side of the top chevron with a pair of jump rings. Add a lobster claw clasp to one side of the necklace and a jump ring to the other.

Braided charm

Kumihimo is the Japanese name for this type of cord made on a braiding wheel. Add beads and attach to your phone or pen case to make it stand out.

You will need

- Phone charm
- Eight 24in. (60cm) lengths of waxed cord thread in each of pink, olive green, cornflower blue, and jade green
- Corrugated card cut into a doughnut shape with 32 equally spaced slots around the edge
- Eight 5mm green beads
- Scissors
- Lighter

1 Thread the charm onto the center of the cords as shown, and fold the ends downward.

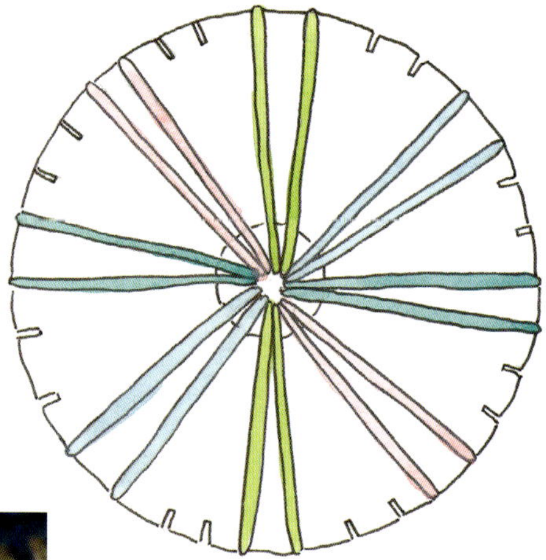

2 Pull the cord ends through the center of the card ring. Hook each length onto the ring so that they are arranged with pairs of cords in the same color opposite each other.

3 Unhook the right-hand cord from the top pair of threads, bring it around, and rehook it to the right of the opposite pair of threads in the same color. This creates a group of three strands.

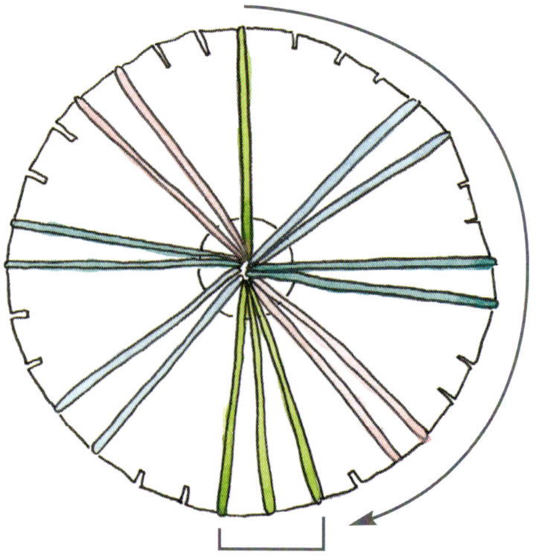

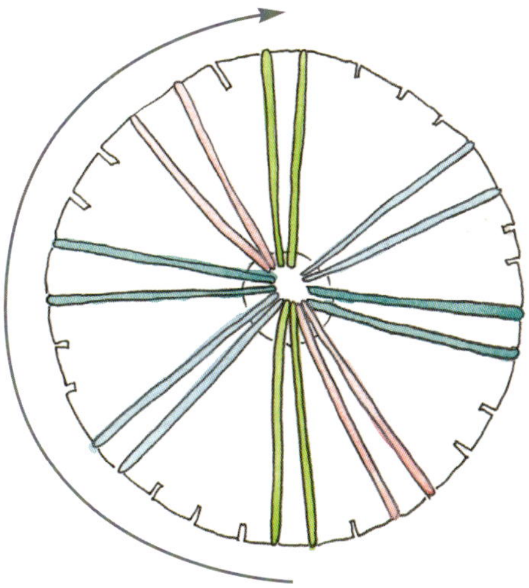

4 Unhook the cord on the left-hand side of the bottom group of three and hook it in the notch to the left of the single cord at the top.

5 Rotate the card ring counter-clockwise by one pair of cords and repeat steps 3 and 4 on the next set of colors. You will see the pattern start to emerge.

6 Braid until the piece measures 2⅜in. (6cm), and then pull it gently off the card ring.

7 Wrap the pink cord around the bottom of the braid and thread up through it. Trim the end. Thread beads onto eight of the remaining cords and then knot to keep in place. Trim all the threads to approximately ⅞in. (2cm) long and seal with a lighter.

TIP

Need a break? Stop when you have three threads on the bottom notch—when you come back to braiding you will know where to start again.

Braided shoelaces

Jazz up your sneakers by making your own shoelaces and fabric liner. This round yarn is ideal—just make sure your braid is thin enough to fit through the eyelets before you make it all!

You will need

- Four 80in. (200cm) lengths of cotton yarn in each of pink, green, turquoise, and cream
- Macramé board and pins
- Clear sticky tape
- Scissors
- Sneakers
- Pencil or fabric marker
- Approximately 12in. (30cm) square of cotton fabric
- Fabric glue

1 Fold the lengths of yarn in half and tie a knot in the top, just below the loop. Attach the loop to your macramé board.

2 Arrange your threads into the following order: blue (A), cream (B), green (C), and pink (D). Move thread A under threads B and C.

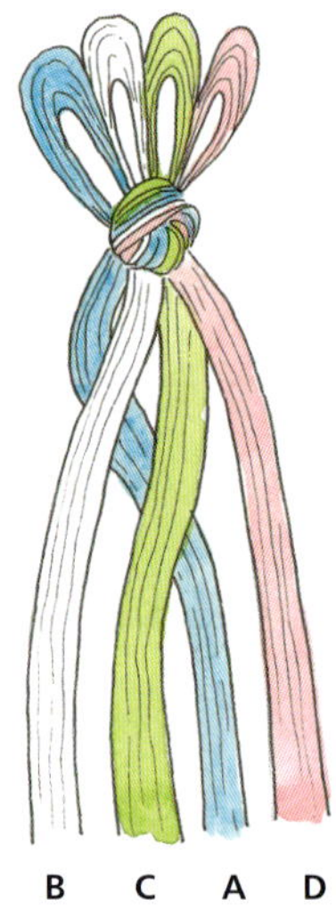

3 Next, move thread A over thread C.

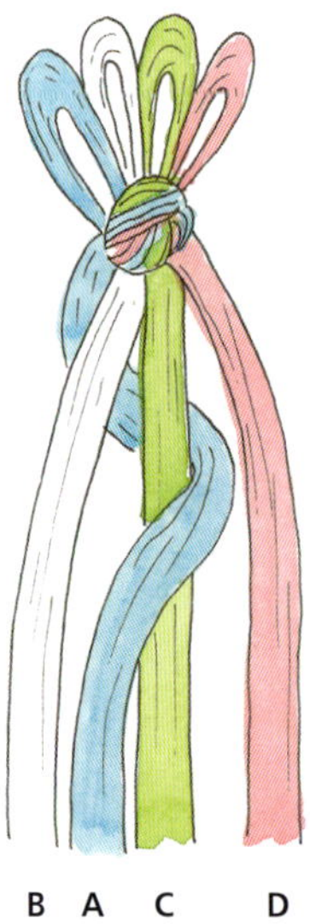

4 Repeat this wrapping sequence on the right side, using thread D. Move it under threads A and C, and then over thread A.

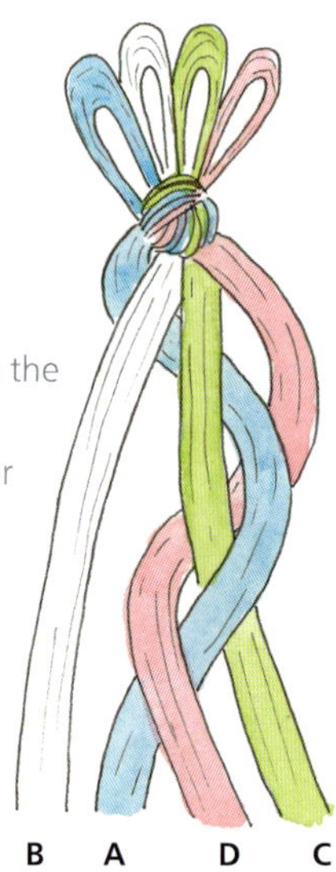

5 Thread B is worked as thread A was in steps 2 and 3, so under threads C and A and then over thread A. Then thread C will be worked as thread D was in step 4, under threads D and B and over thread D, and so on. The outer threads work inward on each step.

6 Repeat steps 2–5 until your braid is as long as the lace that it is replacing.

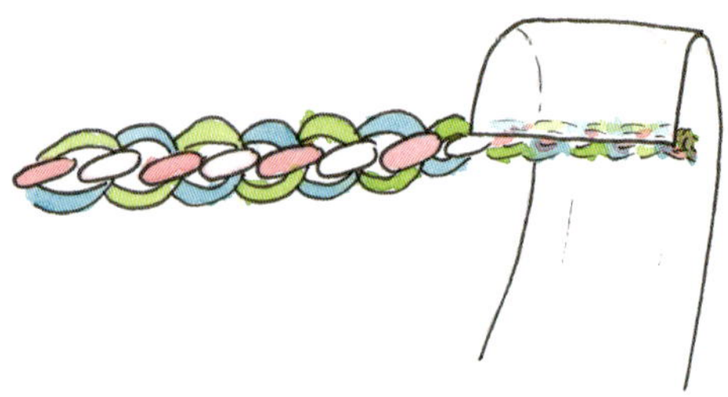

7 Wrap a piece of clear sticky tape tightly around both ends of the cord and cut to create a neat end.

8 Draw around the sole of your shoe onto the cotton fabric for the inside liner of the shoe. Cut out and trim to fit, then stick in place using fabric glue.

9 Thread the lace through the eyelets of your shoe. Repeat steps 1–9 for the other shoe.

Alternating double spiral anklet

This twisting double spiral braid makes an ideal anklet or friendship braid.

You will need

48in. (120cm) of stranded cotton floss in each of pale pink, bright pink, and purple

Macramé board and pins

Scissors

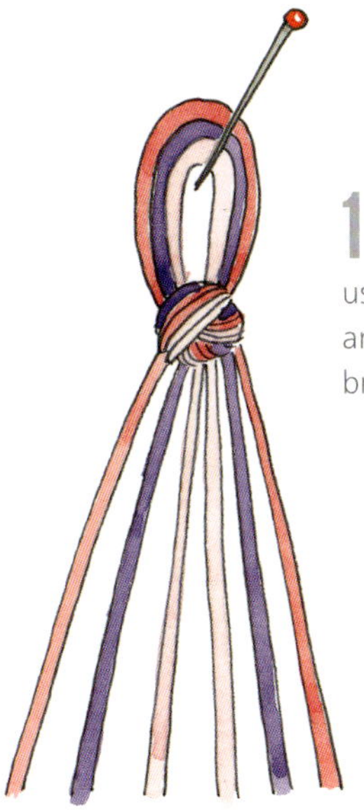

1 Fold the threads in half and tie a knot in the top. Attach this loop to your macramé board using a pin. Arrange the threads so the pale pink are in the center, then the purple, and then the bright pink on the outside.

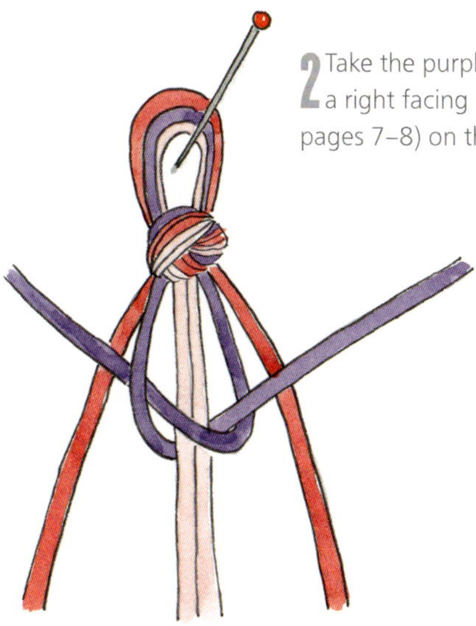

2 Take the purple threads and work a right facing half square knot (see pages 7–8) on the pale pink threads.

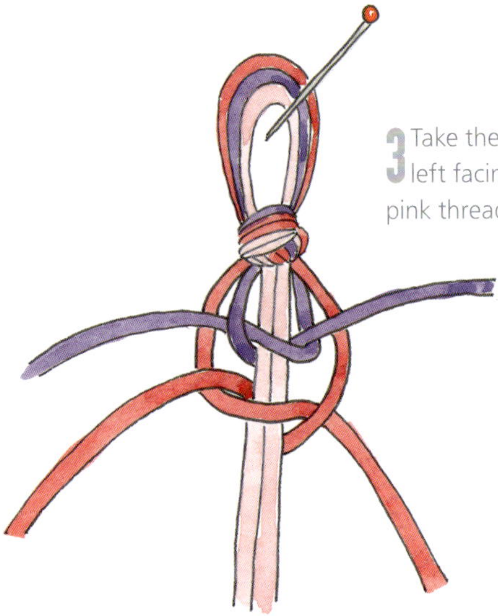

3 Take the bright pink threads and work a left facing half square knot on the pale pink threads.

4 Move the left bright pink thread over the left purple thread and the right bright pink thread under the right purple thread. Then tie the two purple threads into a right facing half square knot.

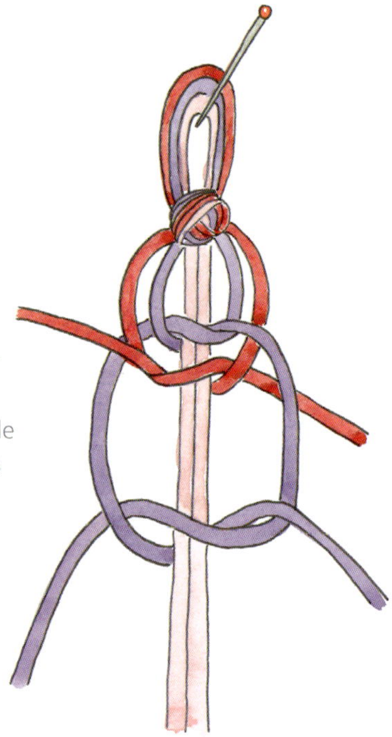

5 Tie a left facing half square knot with the bright pink threads, ensuring that the left bright pink thread goes over the left purple thread and the right bright pink thread goes under the right purple thread.

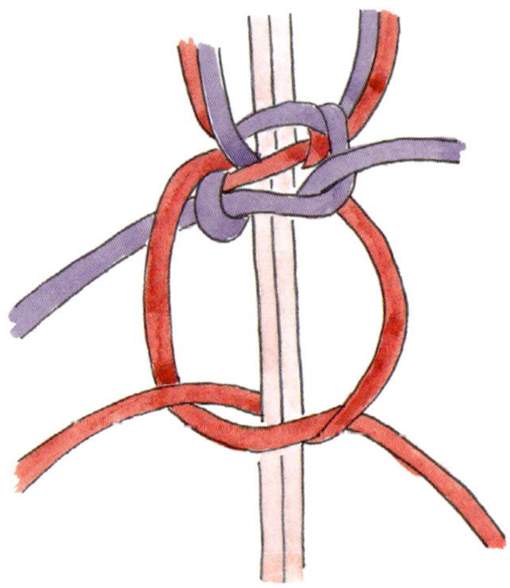

6 Repeat steps 4 and 5 twice more. The threads will twist in opposite directions. Unpin the braid and turn so that the cords you are knotting next are facing you. Then tie a right facing half square knot with the purple threads.

7 Repeat steps 4 and 5 four times, then work step 6 again.

8 Repeat until the braid is approximately 10in. (25cm) long and fits around your ankle, with a bit extra. Tie a knot and trim the ends. To wear, thread the knot through the loop and tie in place.

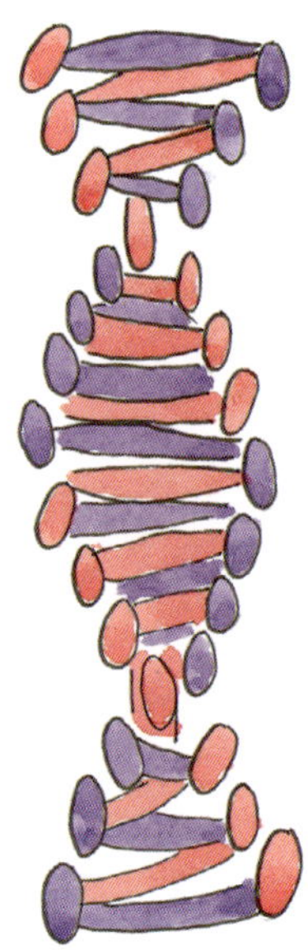

CHAPTER 2:

NATURAL AND HOMESPUN

Tassel necklace

This boho-style necklace would look as good at a festival as it would worn with a simple T-shirt. You could add extra layers of tassels and braids for a more dramatic look.

You will need

- Six 40in. (100cm) lengths of doubled lime green cotton threads
- Macramé board and pins
- Six 48in. (120cm) lengths of doubled lilac cotton threads
- Round silver beads
- Scissors
- Cream, orange, and teal cotton thread
- 6in. (15cm) of thick jute twine
- 10in. (25cm) of thick jute twine
- Four 20in. (50cm) lengths of doubled lime green cotton thread
- Two 20in. (50cm) lengths of doubled teal and orange cotton thread
- Sewing needle
- Cream cotton crochet yarn
- Crochet hook
- Toggle and bar fastening

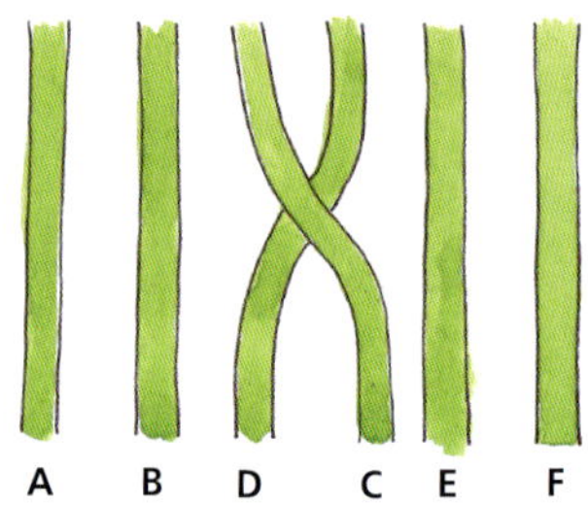

1 Take the six longer green cotton threads and tie them in a knot at one end. Attach this to your macramé board and lay the threads out straight. From the left note them as A, B, C, D, E, and F. Cross thread C over thread D.

2 Then cross thread D over thread B and thread E over thread C.

3 Move thread B over thread E.

4 Weave outer thread A over and under to the right, and thread F under and over to the left—as shown—and then cross A over F in the center.

5 Repeat the weaving of the outer thread into the center, as in step 4, until the braid measures approximately 20in. (50cm).

6 Repeat steps 1–5 with the six longer lilac threads, but for the centre 8in. (20cm) of the braid thread a silver bead onto alternate outer threads and trap them in place in the middle of the braid with the next move.

7 Cut 4in. (10cm) pieces of cream thread and use lark's head knots (see page 7) to attach them to the bottom edge of the central 8in. (20cm) of the lilac braid to make a tassel fringe. Repeat on the central 4in. (10cm) of the lime green braid using the orange thread, adding five teal thread tassels alternately at the very center.

8 To make the feature tassel detail of the necklace, tie knots in either end of the shorter piece of twine and pin to your macramé board as an anchor cord. Add a twist to the longer piece of twine and tie the ends to the anchor cord.

9 Fold the 20in. (50cm) threads in half and use lark's head knots to attach them to either side of the knots in the twine in the following order: green, teal, orange, green on the left side; green, orange, teal, green on the right side.

10 On the left side, take the threads to the right and work vertical clove hitch knots (see page 8) in order down the upper top section of the twisted twine. Repeat on the right side, working reverse vertical clove hitch knots.

11 Take all the threads and work a square knot (see page 7) in the center of the top section of the twisted twine.

12 Now arrange the threads in order again and work vertical and reverse vertical clove hitch knots down the lower top section of the twisted twine on each side.

13 Carry the threads around and down to the bottom section of the twisted twine and repeat steps 10–12 on the bottom section. Trim the thread ends to approx. 1in. (2.5cm). Then fill any remaining empty sections of twisted twine with thread tassels made using lark's head knots.

14 Sew the feature tassel detail to the back at the center of the lilac braid.

15 Knot the lilac and green braids together at each end. To hide the knots create a crochet tube by making a chain of seven (see page 10 for crochet instructions) with the cream yarn. Join to make a circle and then work four rows of single crochet (UK: double crochet). On row 5, decrease to three stitches and then sew the toggle bar to the top. Insert the knot of the braids and sew in place. Repeat to make another crochet piece for the other end to attach the ring of the clasp.

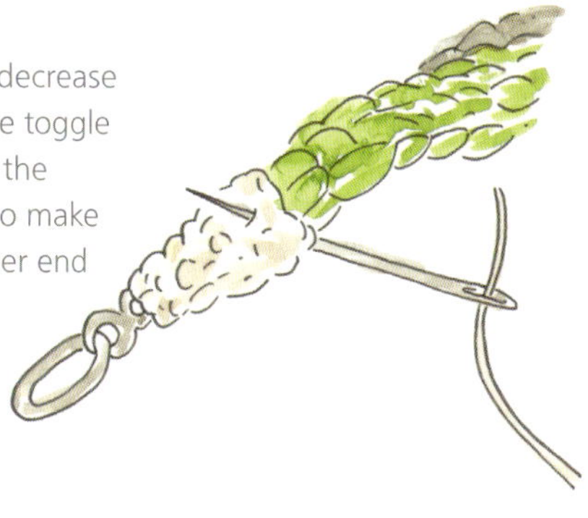

Clove hitch mohair scarf

Create a delicate mohair scarf using a simple clove hitch knot. You can reduce or increase the number of yarn threads to make a thicker or more lacy scarf, depending on whether you are making a spring accessory or a chunky scarf to keep out those winter chills.

You will need

Two 12in. (30cm) lengths of 6 mohair threads:
2 pieces of Debbie Bliss Angel in coral
2 pieces of Debbie Bliss Angel in silver
2 pieces of Debbie Bliss Angel in Lime

Macramé board and pins

Twenty 160in. (4m) sets of 6 mohair threads:
2 pieces of Debbie Bliss Angel in coral
2 pieces of Debbie Bliss Angel in silver
2 pieces of Debbie Bliss Angel in Lime

Scissors

1 Place one of the 12in. (30cm) sets of mohair threads along the top of your macramé board as an anchor cord, and insert the ends into the slots on the sides. Pull tight.

2 Leaving a 4in. (10cm) fringe, tie one of the 160in. (4m) sets of mohair threads onto the anchor cord using a horizontal clove hitch knot (see page 8).

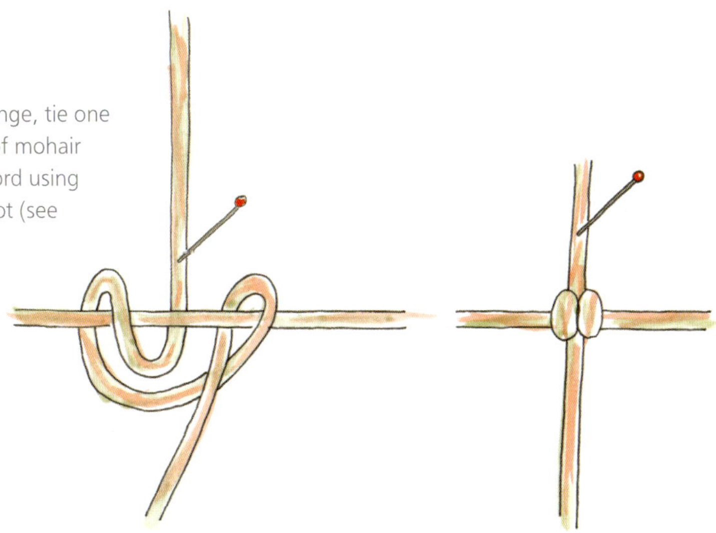

3 Repeat with the remaining 19 cords at even intervals across the anchor cord to create a 'warp' of cords. The first and every sixth cord will be your working cord; the others will be filler cords.

4 Beginning on the left side and using the first cord as your working cord, work five vertical clove hitch knots in a diagonal line down to the right across the next five filler cords.

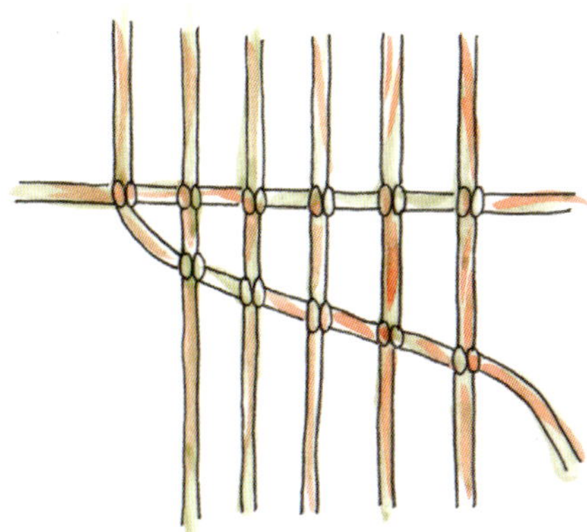

5 Repeat step 4 over the next six cords, again using cord number 1 of the second group as the working cord for that line. On the last group there are eight cords, so again use cord number 1, but this time work seven vertical clove hitch knots.

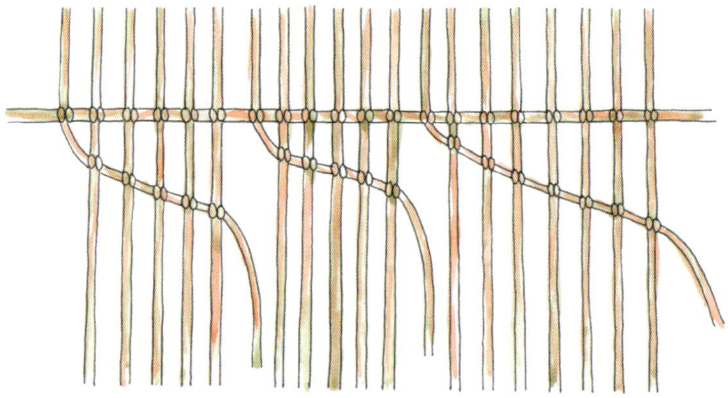

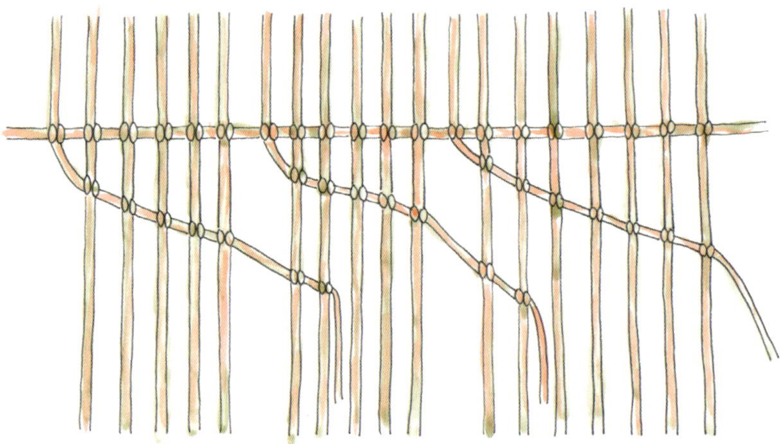

6 Go back to groups 1 and 2 and make two more vertical clove hitch knots in each group, continuing diagonally down to the right so the sections overlap to hold all the threads together.

7 Now repeat steps 4–6 but in reverse, working from the right side to the left. Add a pin at the end of each sideways "V" shape to keep the tension and spacing even, and work the vertical clove hitch knots in the opposite direction.

8 Repeat steps 4–7 until your scarf is the desired length—you will have to keep moving your work up the macramé board.

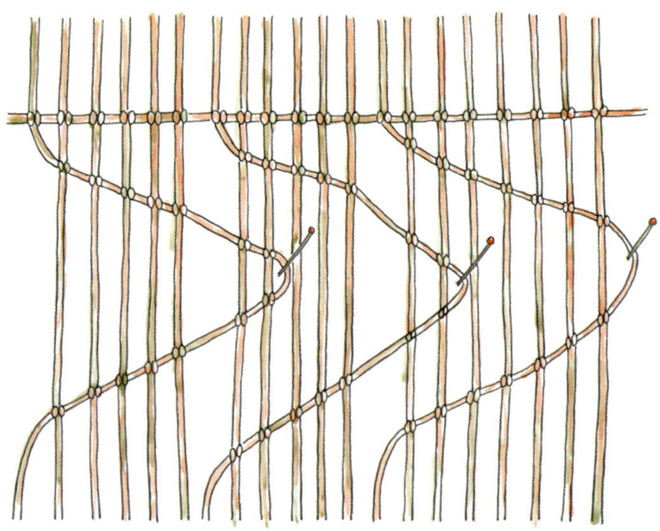

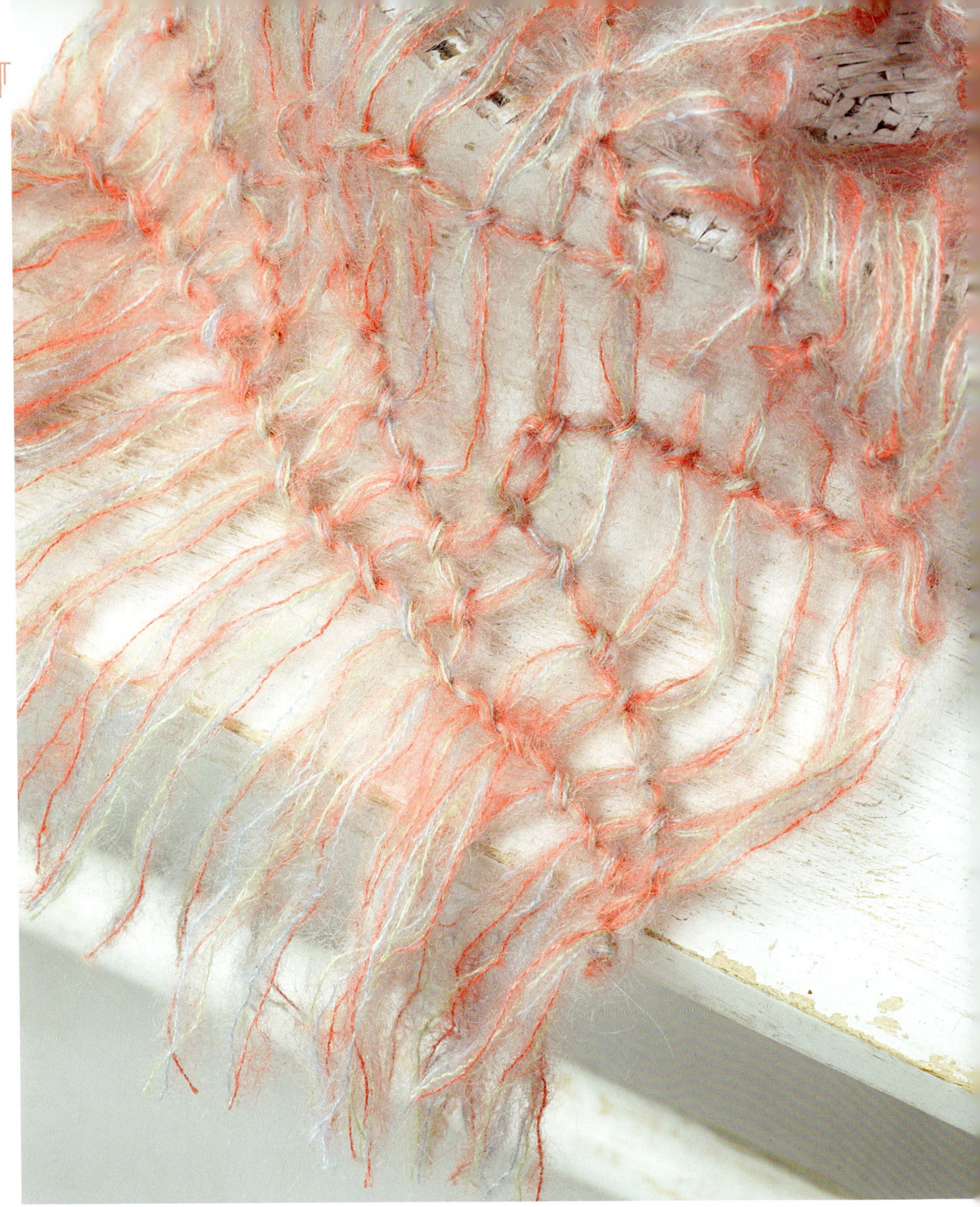

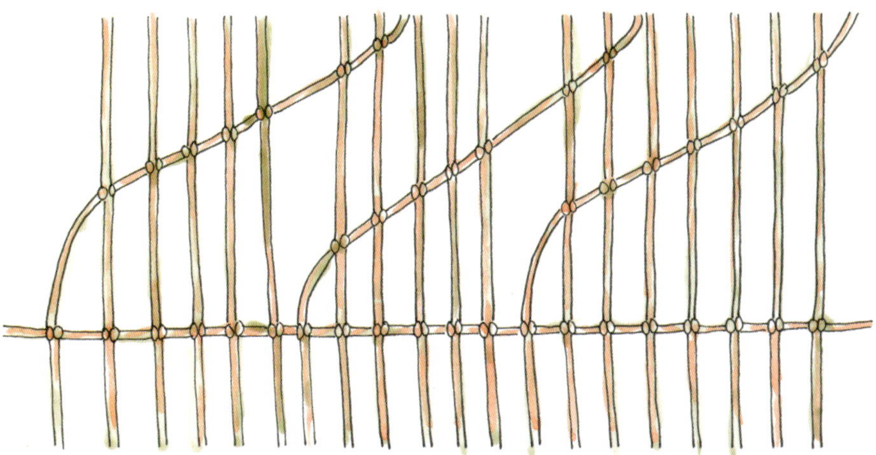

9 To finish, take the second 12in. (30cm) anchor cord and stretch it along the bottom of the board as in step 1. Use this as a filler cord and make a horizontal clove hitch knot with each of the 20 warp cords. Trim the ends to a 4in. (10cm) fringe.

Striped macramé shopper

Shop in style with this funky striped bag—use brightly colored jute cords to update a seventies classic look.

You will need

- Eight 60in. (150cm) lengths of green jute thread
- Four 50in. (125cm) lengths of green jute thread
- Macramé board and pins
- Scissors
- Four 70in. (175cm) lengths of pink jute thread
- Four 70in. (175cm) lengths of mustard jute thread
- Four 70in. (175cm) lengths of turquoise jute thread
- Four 70in. (175cm) lengths of orange jute thread
- Ruler

1 For the first handle you will need four 60in. (150cm) green cords and two 50in. (125cm) green cords. Leaving an 8in. (20cm) end, arrange the cords so there is a long one, short one, two long ones, one short one, and another long one. Make a square knot on the left with cords 1, 2, 3, and 4. Make a second square knot (seepage 7) just below on the right with cords 3, 4, 5, and 6. Continue to work alternating square knots for approximately 6in. (15cm).

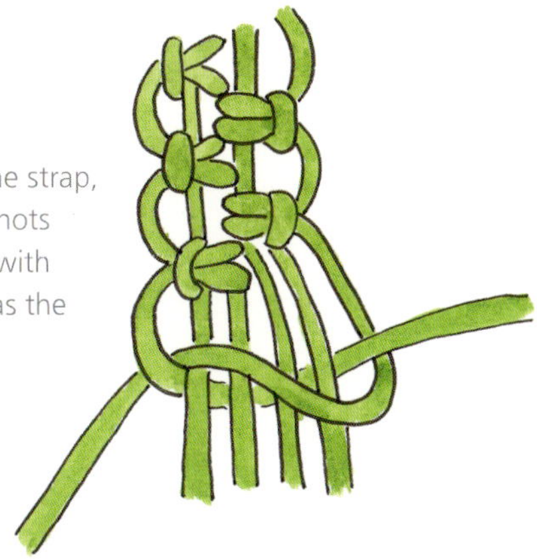

2 For the center of the strap, work two square knots using cords 1 and 6, with the remaining cords as the filler cords.

3 Work another 6in. (15cm) of alternating square knots as in step 1 to make the other half of the first strap. Put to one side and repeat steps 1–3 to make a second handle.

4 Arrange one of the handles into a horseshoe shape and pin to your board. Arrange the threads from the handles so that two from each side cross over in the middle to make a central bar. The remaining four cords from each handle should be stretched outward from the handle. Take your first pink thread and attach to the central bar using a lark's head knot (see page 7).

5 Take the left thread from the lark's head knot and tie another lark's head knot.

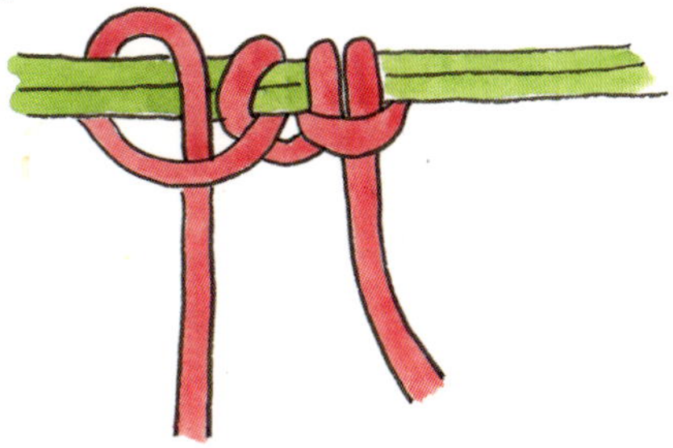

6 Then take the right thread from the original lark's head knot and tie a third lark's head knot to create a solid, neat knot. Push the knot to the left side of the handle, as close as you can.

7 Repeat with another pink thread, pushing it up to the first knot. Then tie two of the mustard threads and finally two more pink threads. They should fill the entire space between the sides of the handle, approximately 6in. (15cm).

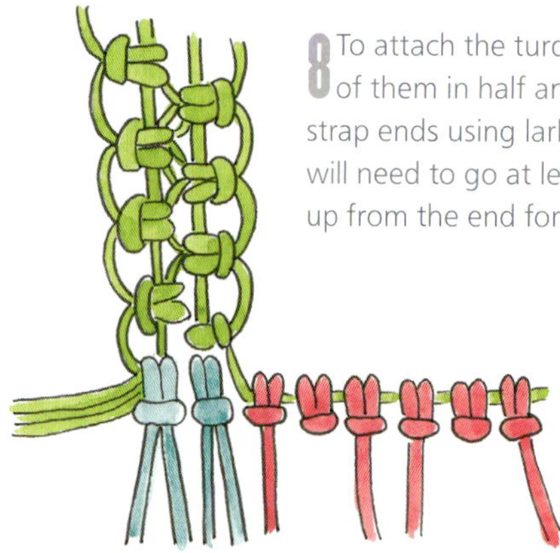

8 To attach the turquoise cords, fold two of them in half and attach them to the strap ends using lark's head knots. You will need to go at least one square knot up from the end for a sturdy knot.

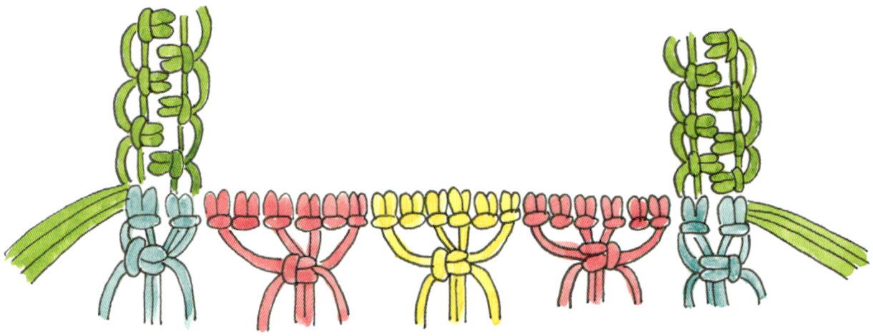

9 Divide the cords into groups of four and work five square knots along just below the top of the bag.

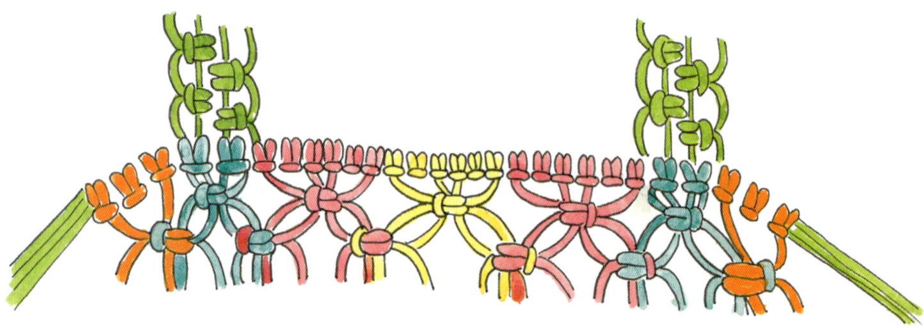

10 Add an orange cord to each end of the bag, on the other side of the handle, in the same way as before. Work six square knots across close to the first row of knots.

11 Add another orange cord to each end and work seven square knots.

12 Add a mustard cord to each end and then put to one side. Repeat steps 4–12 to make the other side of the bag top.

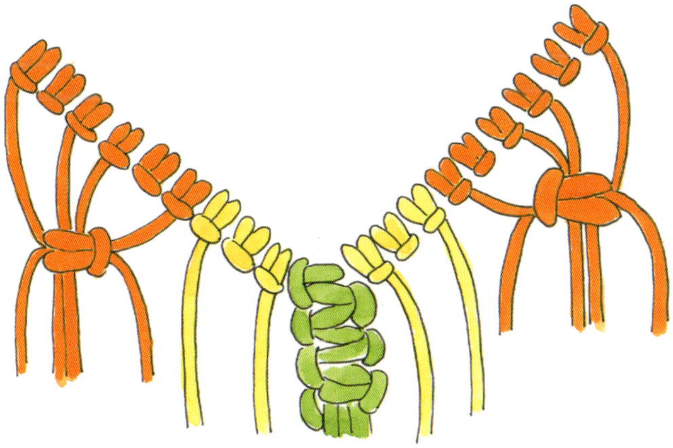

13 To join the sides of the bag, place the pieces together in a V-shape and arrange the threads so that you can make a 1in. (2.5cm) length of square knots. Thread the working cord ends up through the braid and trim all the ends. Repeat on the other side of the bag.

14 Work a final row of tight square knots, eight on each side, to complete the top of the bag.

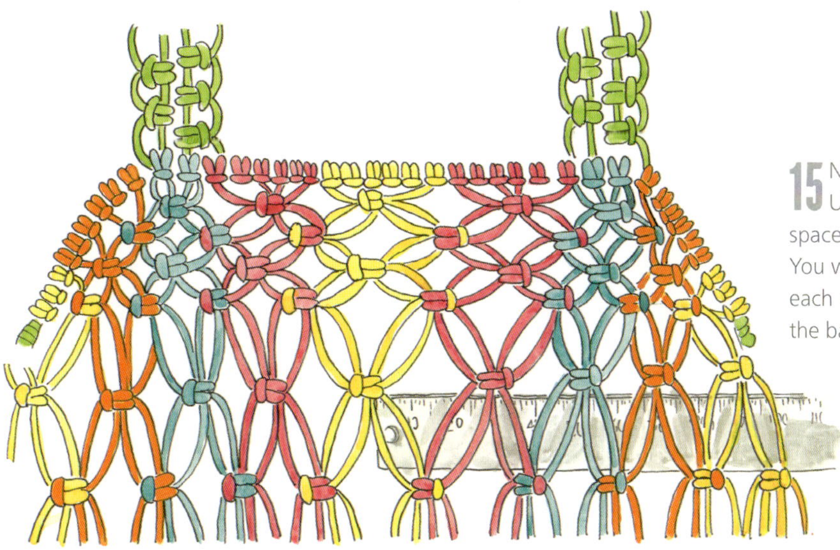

15 Now start making the body of the bag. Use a ruler between each row of knots to space them out and create an open texture. You will have to alternate the four cords on each row to continue the pattern. Repeat until the bag is approximately 16in. (40cm) long.

16 Once your bag is big enough, turn it inside out and tie the ends into knots, ensuring you have a cord from both sides of the bag in each knot. Trim the ends to 1in. (2.5cm) and turn the bag right side out.

Cabochon bracelet

Show off a beautiful semi-precious cabochon stone with this pretty bracelet.

You will need

- 140in. (350cm) of green cotton pearle thread
- Scissors
- Cabochon stone (approx. 1 x ¾in./2.5 x 2cm)
- Eighteen 40in. (100cm) lengths of green cotton cotton perle thread
- 20in. (50cm) length of green cotton perle thread

1 Cut two 22in. (55cm) lengths of green cotton perle thread for the holding cords. Cut two lengths for the working cords that are 12 times the perimeter of the cabochon. The perimeter of my cabochon was 3in. (7.5cm), so my working cords are 36in. (90cm).

2 Attach the holding cords to your macramé board, leaving an 8in. (20cm) end on each. The cords should be wider apart than the side of the cabochon.

3 Attach your first working cord next to the left holding cord, leaving an 8in. (20cm) end again. Work a right-facing lark's head knot (see page 7) on the left cord, then take the bottom end of the left working cord over the right holding cord.

4 Add the second working cord on the other side in the same way, work a left facing lark's head knot on the right cord, and then take the bottom end of the right working cord over the left working and holding cords.

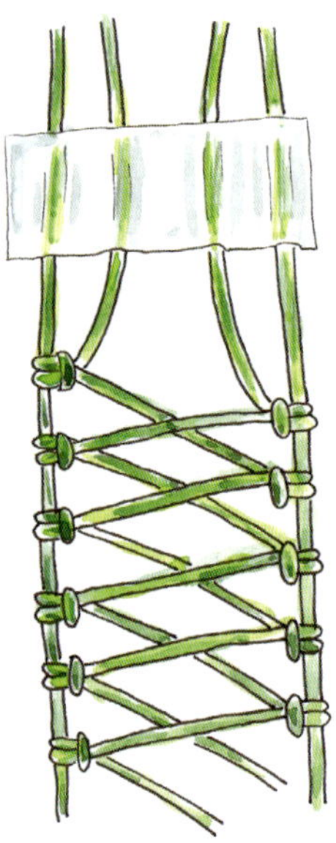

5 Now repeat steps 3 and 4, using the left working cord to make a lark's head knot on the right holding cord, and the right working cord to make one on the left holding cord. Continue knotting on alternate sides until your piece measures approximately ¾in. (2cm) less than the diameter of your cabochon—2in. (5cm) with my particular cabochon. It must be smaller than the perimeter to contain the cabochon once tied.

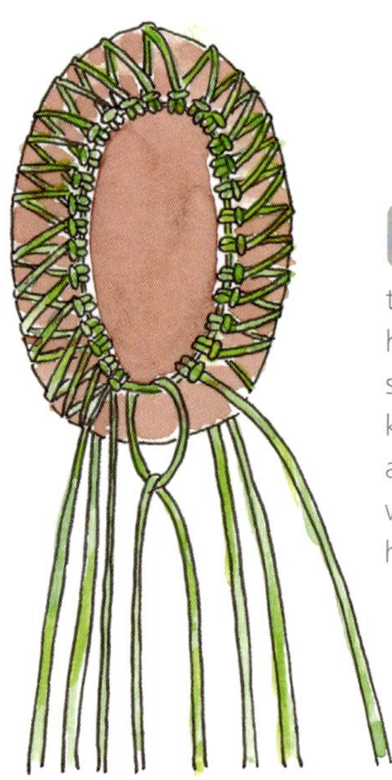

6 Insert your cabochon into the knotted section, and then pull the ends of the holding cord tight to hold the stone in place. Tie a double knot. Turn the cabochon over and repeat on the other side with the ends of the other holding cord.

7 Thread the ends of the working and holding cords into the lark's head knots to neaten, and trim.

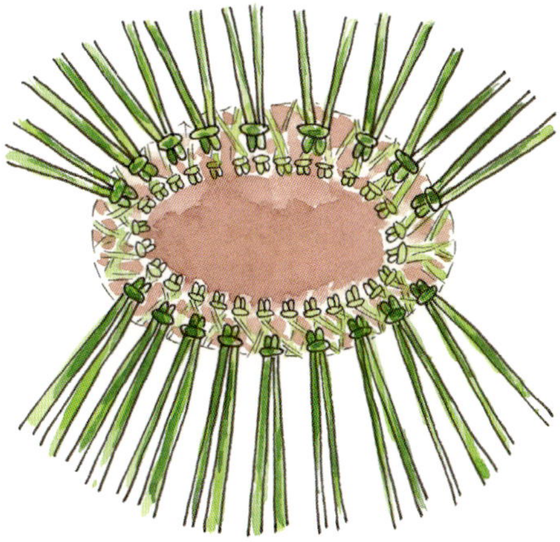

8 Turn the cabochon over so the flat side is facing you. Fold each of the eighteen 40in. (100cm) lengths in half and attach them evenly around the stone using lark's head knots.

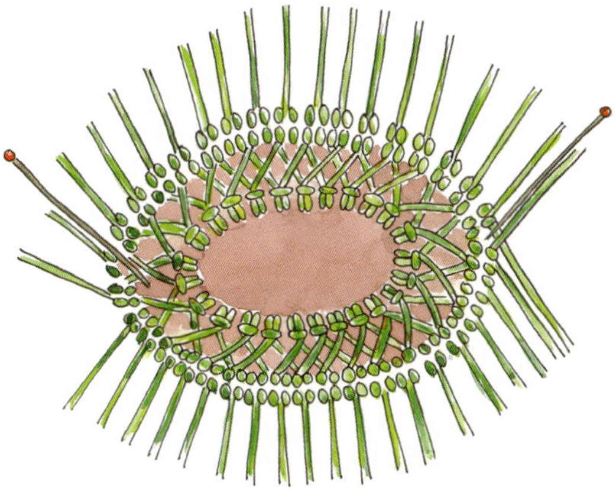

9 Pin the 20in. (50cm) thread to the macramé board so it runs around the edge of the cabochon. Using the cords you attached in step 8, work two rounds of clove hitch knots (see page 8).

10 Now work one end at a time. Starting on the left, and using the first cord as the working cord, work eight clove hitch knots across the other cords into the center. Then, starting on the right, again using the first cord as the working cord, work eight reverse clove hitch knots (see page 8) across the other cords into the center. Join the two sides with a forward knot (see page 6). Repeat twice more.

11 Now work on the central six cords only. Use the left-hand cord of the six to work a clove hitch on each of the next two cords to the right. Use the right-hand cord of the six to work a reverse clove hitch on each of the next two cords to the left, joining to the other side with a forward knot. Repeat eight more times.

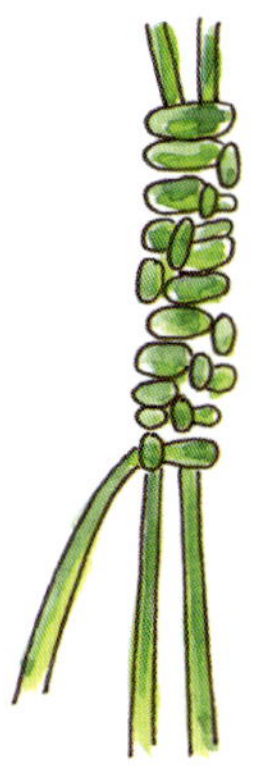

12 Divide the remaining cords on the left into two bunches of three. Take the outer bunch and use the outer cord of this to work a continuous series of forward knots around the other two threads to create a half hitch spiral. Repeat until the spiral measures approximately 1¼in. (3cm).

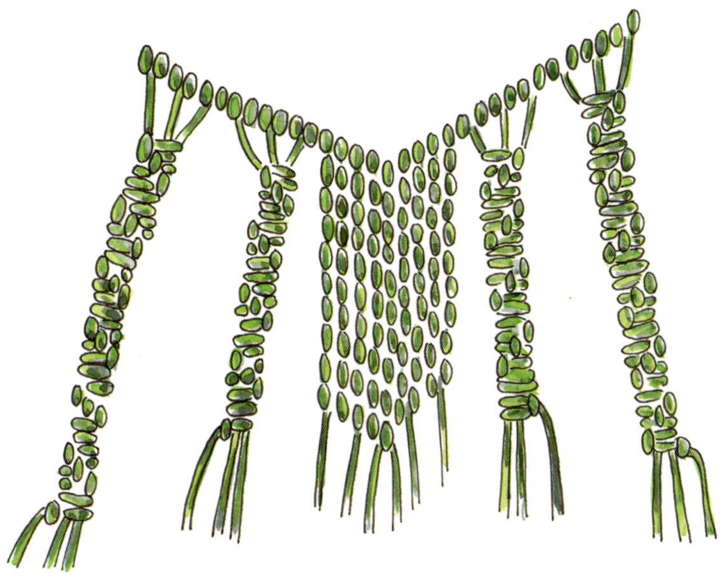

13 Repeat with the inner bunch to make a spiral of approximately ⅞in. (2cm), and then repeat to make two spirals on the other side.

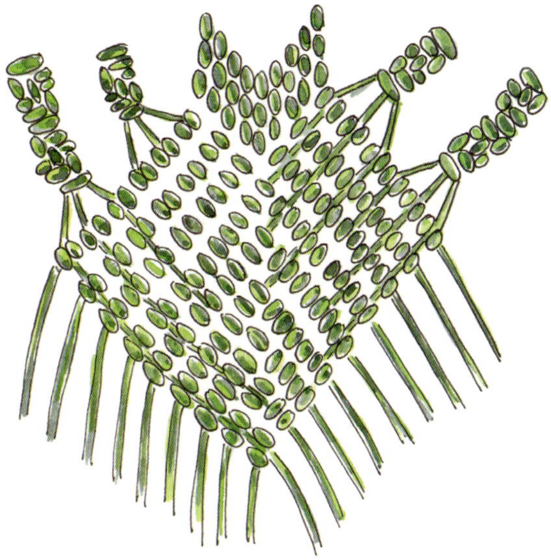

14 Working from the center outward, work reverse clove hitch and clove hitch knots across all the ends to the outer edge. Start with the left cord of the section created in step 11 and use the cords coming from the spirals to make six reverse clove hitch knots. Repeat on the left side to make six clove hitch knots. Repeat with the next two cords. Continue for five more rows, using the central cord of the row as your filler cord and the threads from the row above to make your reverse and clove hitch knots until you create the triangle shape.

15 Now divide the cords into six bunches of three. With the first bunch of three cords work six rows of two forward knots. Repeat with the two remaining left-hand bunches and then repeat on the right side with backward knots (see page 6).

16 Finally, work three rows of clove hitch knots into the center from the left, and three rows of reverse clove hitch knots into the center from the right. Join the rows with forward knots.

17 Divide each side into three bunches and braid for approximately 3in. (7.5cm). Finish with a knot.

18 Repeat steps 10 to 16 on the other side of the cabochon.

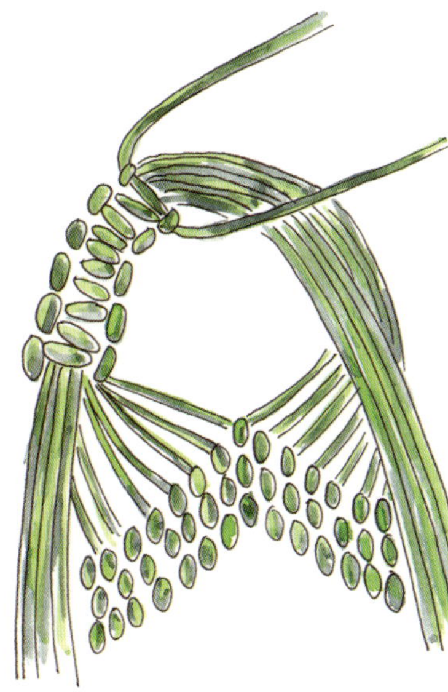

19 To make the loop at the other end, fold the cord ends over each other and then take two outer cords and work square knots (see page 7) around the loop to the end. Thread the working cords up through the knots. Trim all the cord ends.

Braided ribbon straw hat

Add a touch of color to your summer straw hat with this intricate braid. If you find this too complicated, try searching for simpler designs online.

You will need

- Six 120in. (300cm) lengths of cream stranded floss
- Two 120in. (300cm) lengths of orange stranded floss
- 120in. (300cm) length of lime green stranded floss
- 120in. (300cm) length of mid-green stranded floss
- 120in. (300cm) length of dark green stranded floss
- 120in. (300cm) length of yellow stranded floss
- Macramé board
- Pins
- Scissors
- Straw hat
- Ribbon
- Superglue or needle and thread

1 Fold all the threads in half, tie in a knot at the loop end and pin to your macramé board so the strands run in the following order left to right: cream, orange, lime green, cream, cream, mid-green, dark green, cream, cream, orange, yellow, cream, cream, yellow, orange, cream, cream, dark green, mid-green, cream, cream, lime green, orange, cream.

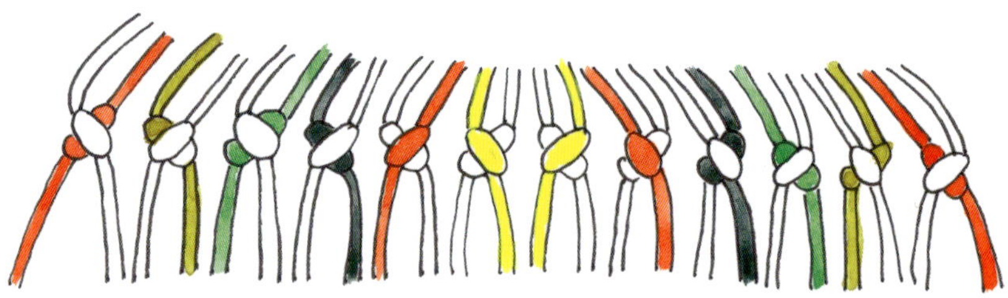

2 **Row 1**: Work a forward knot (FK; see page 6) with cream (C) on orange (O), a backward knot (BK; see page 6) with cream (C) on lime green (LG), a forward knot (FK) with cream (C) on mid-green (MG), a backward knot (BK) with cream (C) on dark green (DG), a backward knot (BK) with orange (O) on cream (C), a forward knot (FK) with yellow (Y) on cream (C), a backward knot (BK) with yellow (Y) on cream (C), a forward knot (FK) with orange (O) on cream (C), a forward knot (FK) with cream (C) on dark green (DG), a backward knot (BK) with cream (C) on mid-green (MG), a forward knot (FK) with cream (C) on lime green (LG), and a backward knot (BK) with cream (C) on orange (O).

3 **Row 2**: Skip an O thread, work a FK with C on C, work a left facing lark's head knot (LLHK; see page 7) with LG on MG, work a FK with C on C, work a right facing lark's head knot (RLHK) with O on DG, work a FK with C on C, work a FK with Y on Y, work a FK with C on C, work a LLHK with O on DG, work a FK with C on C, work a RLHK with LG on MG, work a FK with C on C, skip an O thread.

4 **Row 3**: Work a BK with C on O, work a BK with LG on C, work a BK with C on MG, work a FK with C on DG, work a BK with C on O, work a BK with Y on C, work a FK with Y on C, work a FK with C on O, work a BK with C on DG, work a FK with C on MG, work a FK with LG on C, work a FK with C on O.

5 **Row 4**: Skip a C thread, work a RLHK with LG on O, work a FK with C on C, work a LLHK with MG on DG, work a FK with C on C, work a LLKH with O on Y, work a FK with C on C, work a RLHK with O on Y, work a FK with C on C, work a RLHK with MG on DG, work a FK with C on C, work a LLHK with LG on O, skip a C thread.

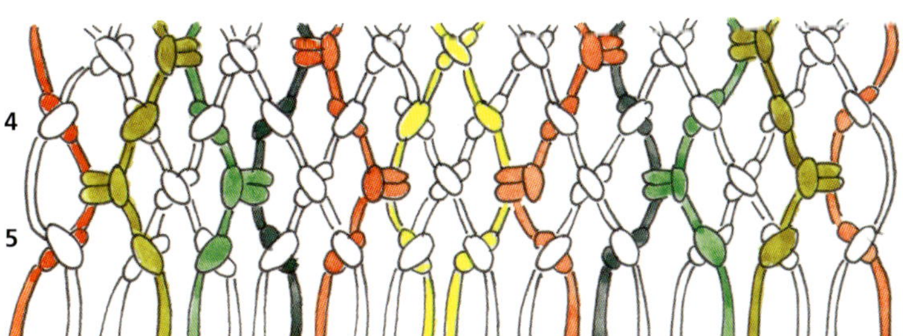

6 **Row 5**: Work a FK with C on O, work a FK with LG on C, work a BK with MG on C, work a BK with C on DG, work a FK with C on O, work a BK with C on Y, work a FK with C on Y, work a FK with C on DG, work a FK with MG on C, work a BK with LG on cream, work a BK with C on O.

7 **Row 6**: Skip an O thread, work a FK with C on C, work a RLHK with MG on LG, work a FK with C on C, work a LLHK with DG on O, work a LLHK with C on C, work a FK with Y on Y, work a RLHK with C on C, work a RLHK with DG on O, work a FK with C on C, work a LLHK with MG on LG, work a FK with C on C, skip an O thread.

8 **Row 7**: Work a BK with C on O, work a FK with C on LG, work a FK with MG on C, work a BK with DG on C, work a BK with C on O, work a LLHK with C on Y, work a RLHK with C on Y, work a FK with C on O, work a FK with DG on C, work a BK with MG on C, work a BK with C on LG, work a FK with C on O.

9 **Row 8**: Skip a C thread, work a RLHK with LG on O, work a FK with C on C, work a LLHK with MG on DG, work a RLHK with C on C, work a LLHK with O on C, work a FK with Y on Y, work a RLHK with O on C, work a LLHK with C on C, work a RLHK with MG on DG, work a FK with C on C, work a LLHK with LG on O, skip a C thread.

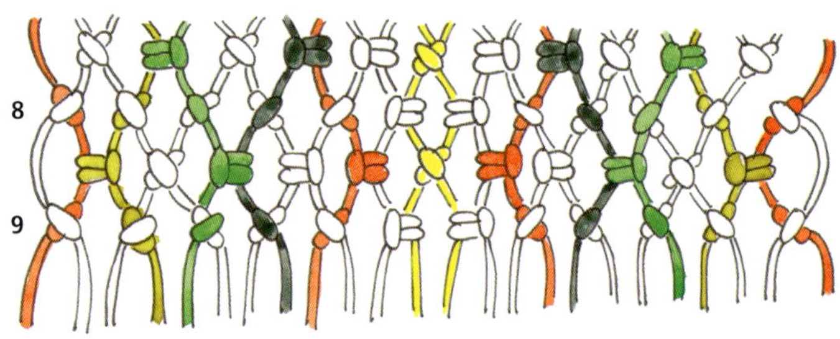

10 **Row 9**: Work a FK with C on O, work a BK with C on LG, work a BK with MG on C, work a FK with DG on C, work a FK with C on O, work a LLHK with C on Y, work a RLHK with C on Y, work a BK with C on O, work a BK with DG on C, work a FK with MG on C, work a FK with C on LG, work a BK with C on O.

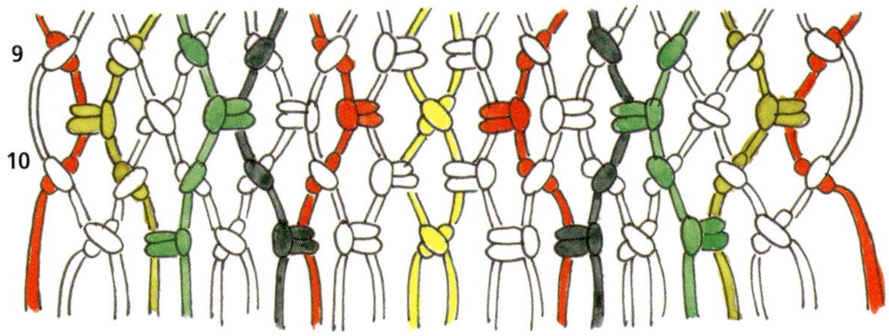

11 **Row 10**: Skip an O thread, work a FK with C on C, work a RLHK with MG on LG, work a FK with C on C, work a LLHK with DG on O, work a LLHK with C on C, work a FK with Y on Y, work a RLHK with C on C, work a RLHK with DG on O, work a FK with C on C, work a LLHK with MG on LG, work a FK with C on C, skip an O thread.

12 **Row 11**: Work a BK with C on O, work a BK with LG on C, work a FK with MG on C, work a FK with C on DG, work a BK with C on O, work a FK with C on Y, work a BK with C on Y, work a FK with C on O, work a BK with C on DG, work a BK with MG on C, work a FK with LG on C, work a FK with C on O.

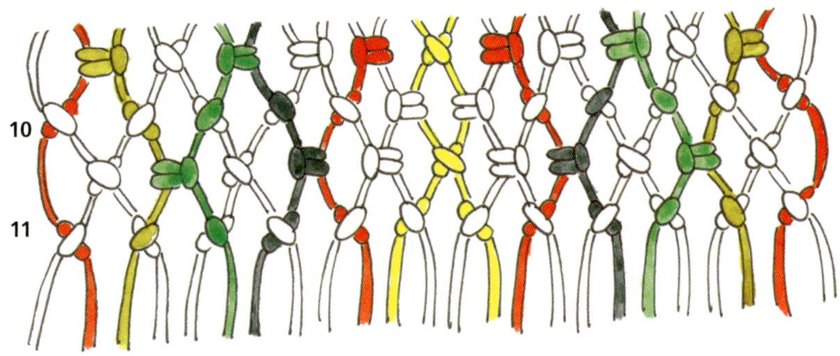

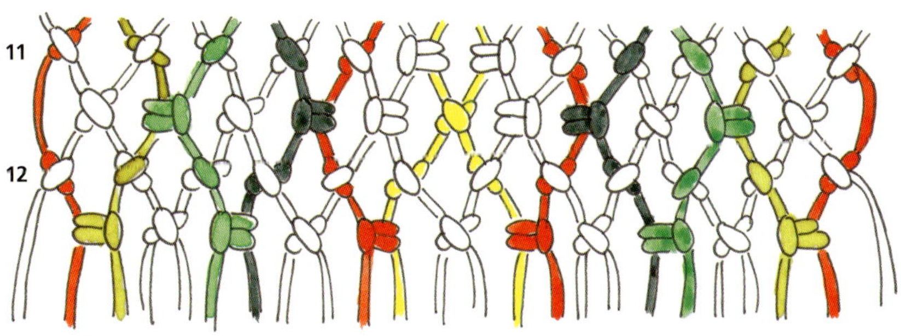

13 **Row 12**: Skip a C thread, work a RLHK with LG on O, work a FK with C on C, work a LLHK with MG on DG, work a FK with C on C, work a LLHK with O on Y, work a FK with C on C, work a RLHK with O on Y, work a FK with C on C, work a RLHK with MG on DG, work a FK with C on C, work a LLHK with LG on O, skip a C thread.

14 **Row 13**: Work a FK with C on O, work a FK with LG on C, work a FK with C on MG, work a BK with C on DG, work a FK with C on O, work a FK with Y on C, work a BK with Y on C, work a FK with C on DG, work a BK with C on MG, work a BK with LG on C, work a BK with C on O.

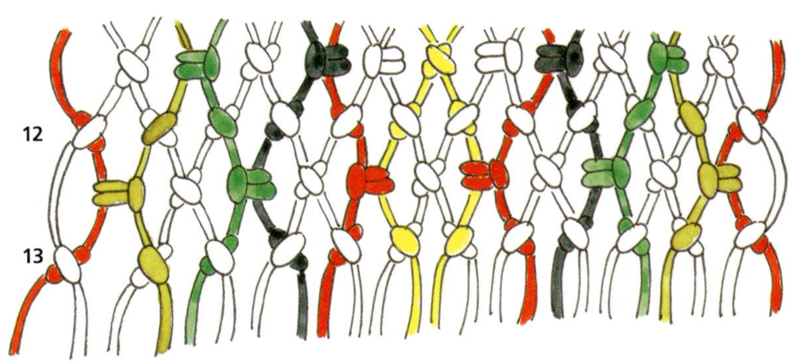

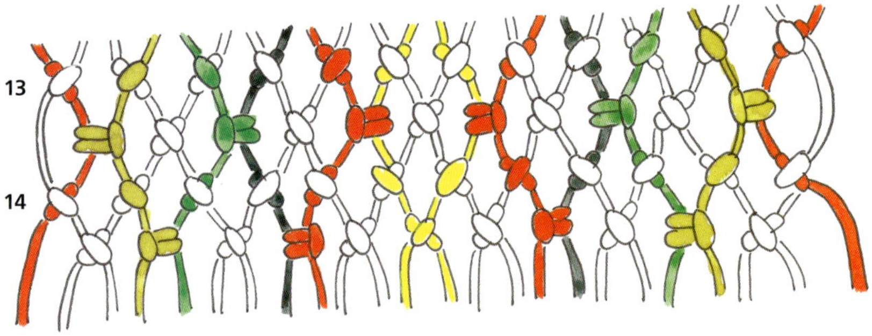

15 **Row 14**: Skip an O thread, work a FK with C on C, work a LLHK with LG on MG, work a FK with C on C, work a RLHK with O on DG, work a FK with C on C, work a BK with Y on Y, work a FK with C on C, work a LLHK with O on DG, work a FK with C on C, work a RLHK with LG on MG, work a FK with C on C, skip an O thread.

17 **Row 15**: Work a BK with C on O, work a FK with C on LG, work a BK with C on MG, work a FK with C on DG, work a FK with O on C, work a BK with Y on C, work a FK with Y on C, work a BK with O on C, work a BK with C on DG, work a FK with C on MG, work a BK with C on LG, work a FK with C on O.

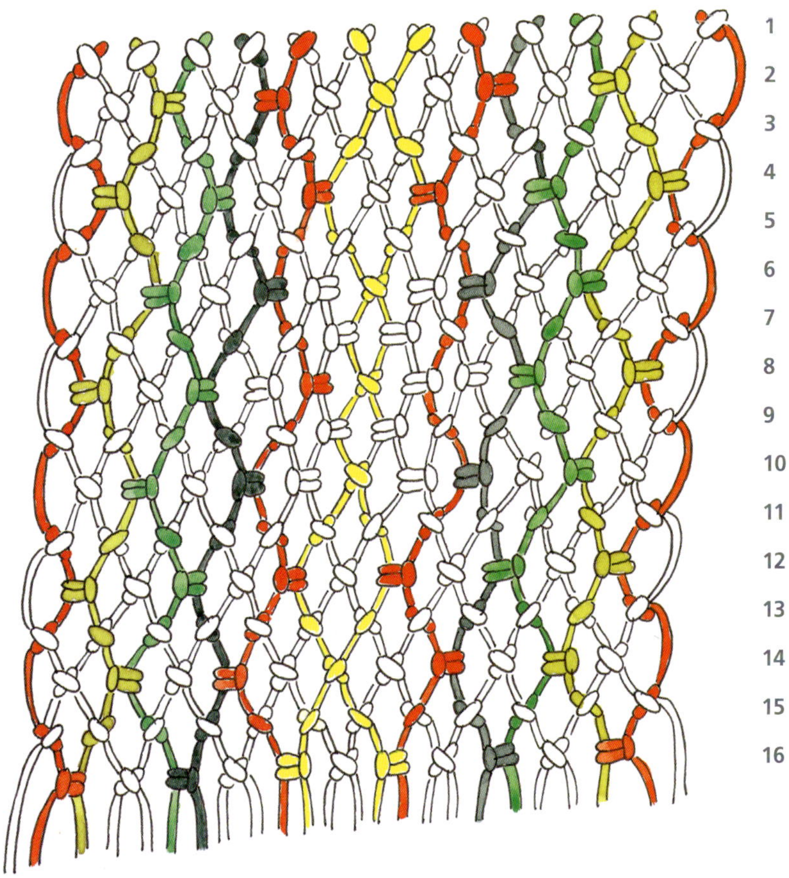

16 **Row 16**: Skip a C thread, work a LLHK with O on LG, work a FK with C on C, work a RLHK with DG on MG, work a FK with C on C, work a RLHK with Y on O, work a FK with C on C, work a LLHK with Y on O, work a FK with C on C, work a LLHK with DG on MG, work a FK with C on C, work a RLHK with O on LG, skip a C thread.

18 Repeat steps 2–17 until your braid is long enough to go around the hat.

19 Thread both ends of the braid through the hat and tie in knots on the inside to secure in place (the ribbon inside the hat should hide all the knots).

20 Make a ribbon bow and attach to cover the join using superglue, or by stitching in place.

Macramé pebble pendants

Turn the pretty pebbles you find on long walks into stunning pendant necklaces by encasing them in macramé. Try using bright color-waxed cord for a contrasting effect.

You will need

Pink pendant

- 200in. (5m) length of 0.1mm diameter pink waxed cotton cord
- 1 black pebble
- Scissors
- Clear sticky tape
- Leather cord necklace

Green pendant

- Eight 40in. (100cm) lengths of 0.1mm diameter olive green waxed cord
- 1 cream stone
- Scissors
- Pins
- Leather cord necklace

Turquoise pendant

- Twelve 48in. (120cm) lengths of 0.1mm diameter turquoise waxed cord
- 1 black pebble
- Scissors
- Superglue
- Leather cord necklace

Pink pendant

1 Cut two pieces of cord 22in. (55cm) long for the holding cords. Cut two working cords that are 12 times the perimeter of the stone. My stone was 1¾ x 2¼in. (4.5 x 5.5cm) with a perimeter of 6in. (15cm), so my working cords are 72in. (180cm).

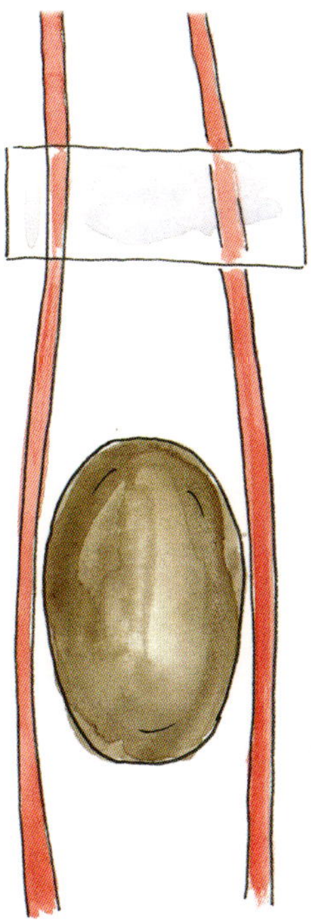

2 Attach the holding cords to your work surface with tape, leaving an 8in. (20cm) end on each. The cords should be wider apart than the width of the stone.

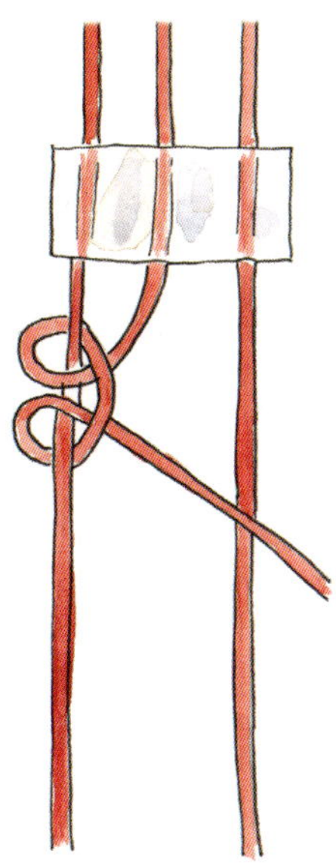

3 Attach your first working cord next to the left holding cord, leaving an 8in. (20cm) end again. Work a right-facing lark's head knot (see page 7) on the left cord, then take the bottom end of the left working cord over the right holding cord.

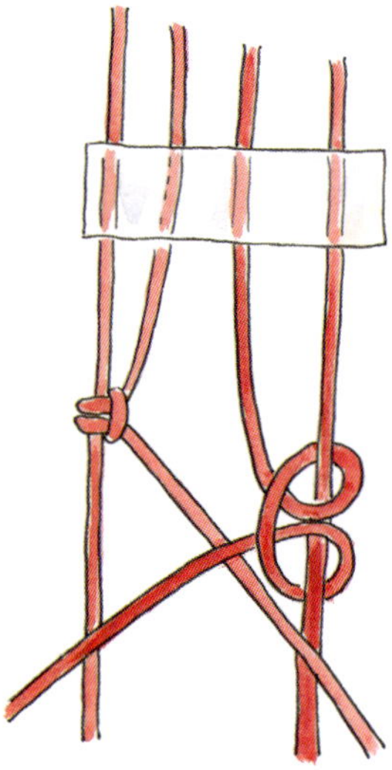

4 Add the second working cord on the other side in the same way, work a left facing lark's head knot on the right cord, and then take the bottom end of the right working cord over the left working and holding cords.

5 Now repeat steps 3 and 4, using the left working cord to make a lark's head knot on the right holding cord, and the right working cord to make one on the left holding cord. Continue knotting on alternate sides until your piece measures approximately ¾in. (2cm) less than the diameter of your stone—5¼in. (13cm) with my particular stone. It must be smaller than the perimeter to contain the stone once tied.

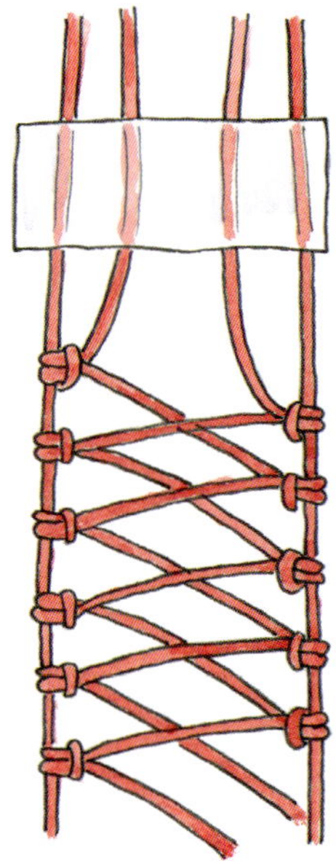

6 Insert your pebble into the knotted section and pull the ends of the holding cord tight to hold the stone in place. Tie a double knot. Turn the stone over and repeat on the other side with the ends of the other holding cord.

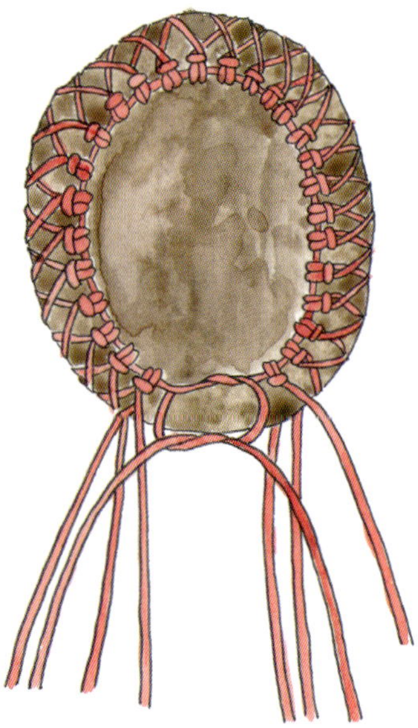

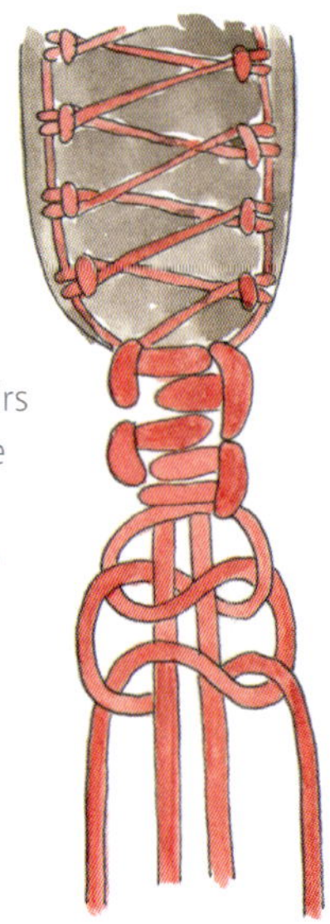

7 Turn the stone on its side and arrange the cords so the two pairs of holding cords are on the outside and the four working cords are in the center. Work square knots (see page 7) for 2in. (5cm).

8 Fold this knotted section in half and thread the ends through the center to create a hanging loop. Trim the excess.

9 Thread the leather cord through the loop on the pendant to complete.

Green pendant

1 Cut eight pieces of waxed cord ten times the diameter of your stone. My stone was 2⅜ x 1¼in. (6 x 3cm) with a diameter of 3¼in. (8cm), so my cords are 32in. (80cm).

2 Now create a zeppelin bend knot (see page 9) to join the threads together; first divide the cords into two sets of four. Bend the sets into two overlapping loops as shown, pinning in place.

3 Take the top cords of the upper loop and thread them under and up through both loops.

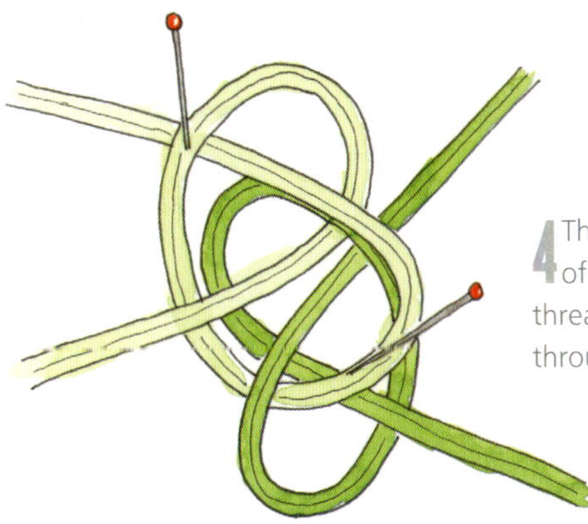

4 Then take the lower cords of the bottom loop and thread them over and down through both loops.

5 Gently pull on all four sets of ends to tighten the knot.

6 Tape the knot to the top of the stone so there are four cords coming off at each corner.

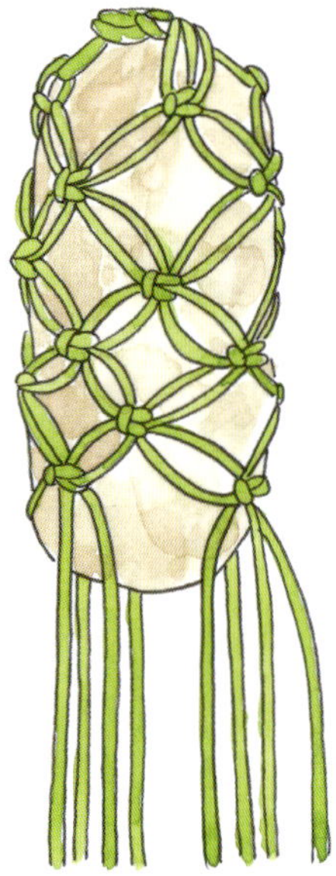

7 Work a square knot in each set of four cords. Leave a space, then make a second round of square knots using the two outer cords from adjacent sets. Continue in this way, spacing the knots to create a lattice tube down the stone.

8 Gather all the cords together at the bottom of the stone and divide into four sets of four cords. Use these to work square knots for 2in. (5cm). Repeat steps 8 and 9 of the pink pendant to complete.

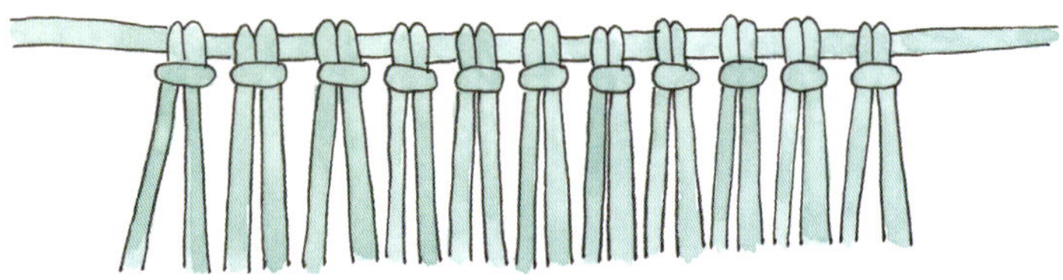

Turquoise pendant

1 Attach 11 of the cords to the 12th one using lark's head knots (see page 7).

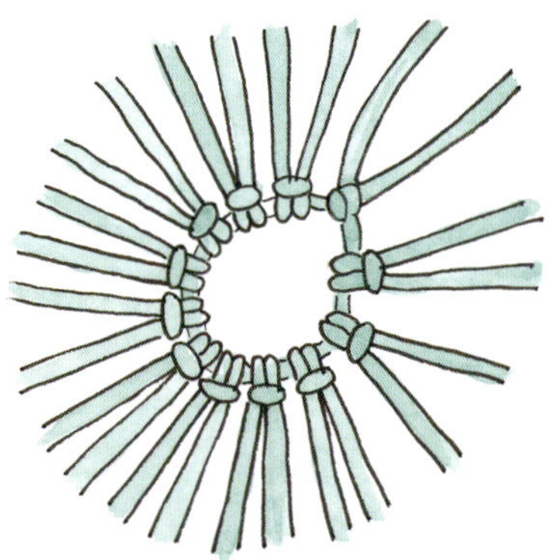

2 Tie the ends of the 12th cord together to make a ring.

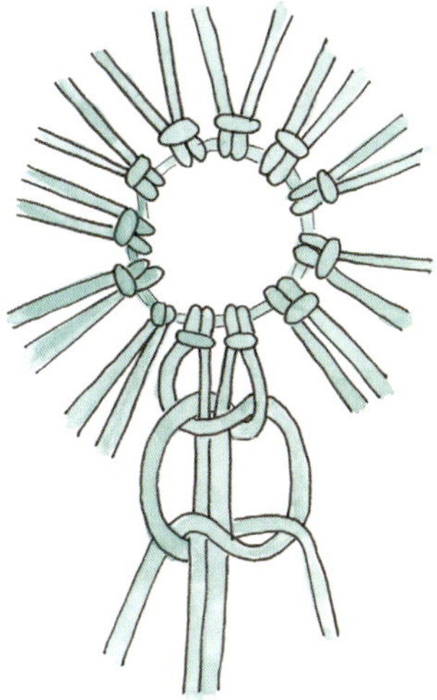

3 Take four of the cords and use them to tie a square knot (see page 7).

4 Keep tying left facing square knots until the spoke is 2in. (5cm) long. Repeat on the other threads so there are six spokes coming from the central ring. Place over the pebble—my pebble was 2⅜in. (6cm) in diameter.

5 Now take the two outer threads from two adjacent spokes and tie a row of square knots.

6 Repeat for three more rows, each row getting tighter to keep the pebble in place.

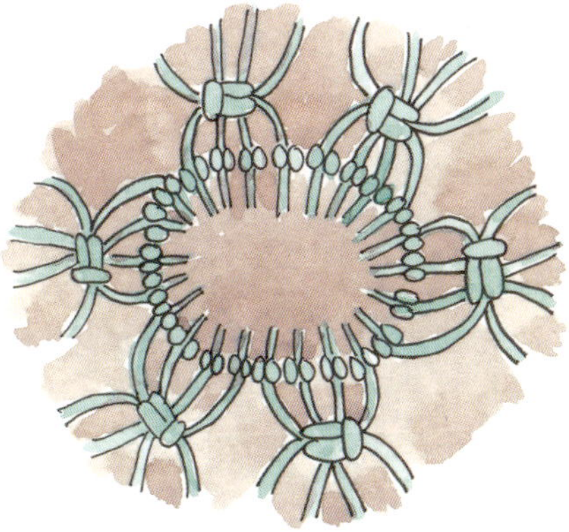

7 Using one of the cords as a filler cord, work a ring of clove hitch knots (see page 8) to make a neat finish. Trim the threads and secure with superglue.

8 Thread the pebble onto the leather cord to complete.

Macramé collar

Add a quirky removable collar to a plain tee or dress. This pretty macramé collar has a crochet flower detail.

You will need

- Rico Creative Cotton Aran weight in mustard, gray, pink, and khaki
- Macramé board and pins
- Scissors
- US size 7 (4mm) crochet hook
- Needle and thread

1 Cut three 56in. (140cm) lengths of mustard yarn and tie together at one end in a knot. Pin to your macramé board and braid the entire length.

2 Pin the central section of the braid to your board.

3 Cut 42 lengths of gray yarn, each 40in (100cm) long. Take a gray cord and attach to the central bar using a lark's head knot (see page 7).

4 Take the left thread from the lark's head knot and tie another lark's head knot.

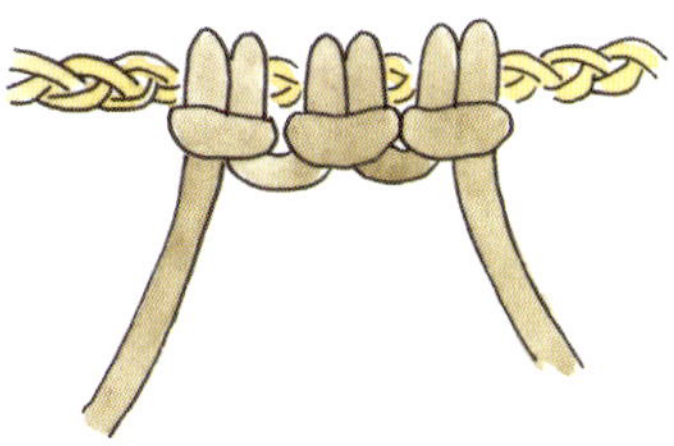

5 Then take the right thread from the original lark's head knot and tie a third lark's head knot to the right to create a solid, neat knot. Push the knot to the left, as close as you can to the left pin.

6 Repeat with the remaining gray cords.

7 Now start braiding. Divide the cord ends into seven groups of 12 and note each set as 1–12 as shown. Working with the first group, take cords 3 and 4 and work a clove hitch knot (see page 8) on cord 4 using cord 3. Repeat using cords 9 and 10. Repeat the knotting sequence on each of the other six groups.

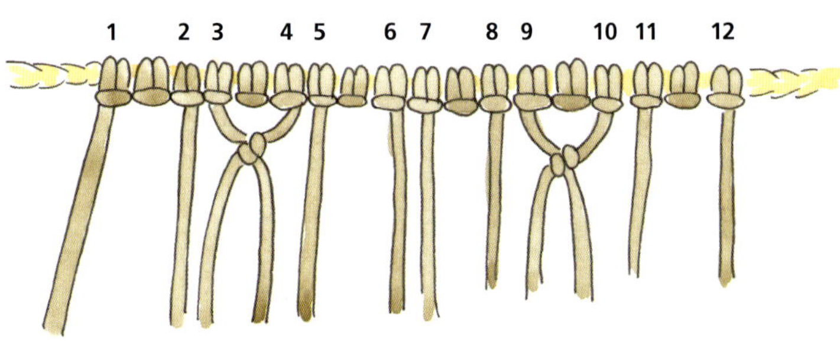

8 Take cord 2 and work a clove hitch knot on cord 4, then use cord 5 to work a reverse clove hitch knot (see page 8) on cord 3. Take cord 8 and work a clove hitch knot on cord 10, then take cord 11 and work a reverse clove hitch knot on cord 9. Repeat the knotting sequence on each of the other six groups.

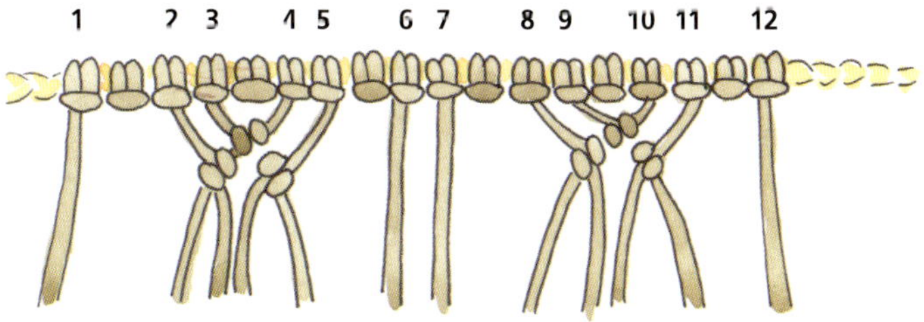

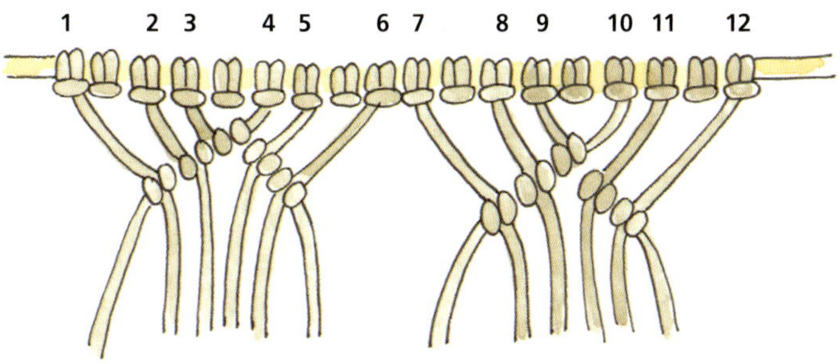

9 Take cord 1 and work a clove hitch knot on cord 4, then use cord 6 to work a reverse clove hitch knot on cord 3. Take cord 7 and work a clove hitch knot on row 10, then take cord 12 and work a reverse clove hitch knot on cord 9. Repeat the knotting sequence on each of the other six groups.

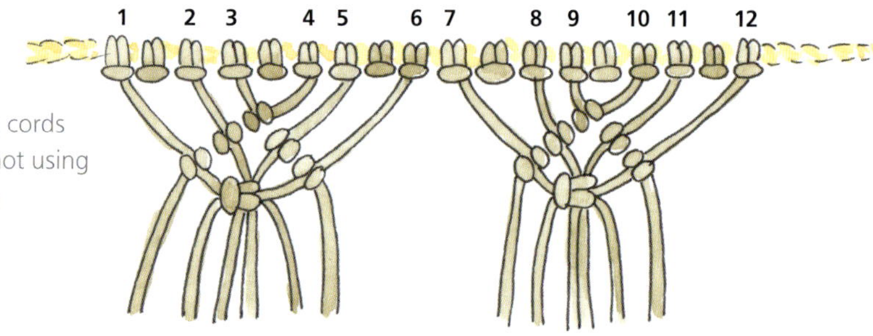

10 Work a square knot (see page 7) using cords 1, 2, 5, and 6. Work another square knot using cords 8, 9, 11, and 12. Repeat the knotting sequence on each of the other six groups.

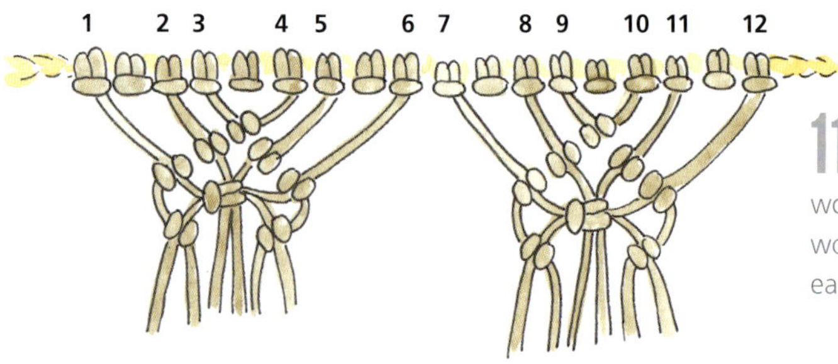

11 Take cord 1 and work a reverse clove hitch knot on cord 4, then use cord 6 to work a clove hitch knot on cord 3. Take cord 7 and work a reverse clove hitch knot on row 10, then take cord 12 and work a clove hitch knot on cord 9. Repeat the knotting sequence on each of the other six groups.

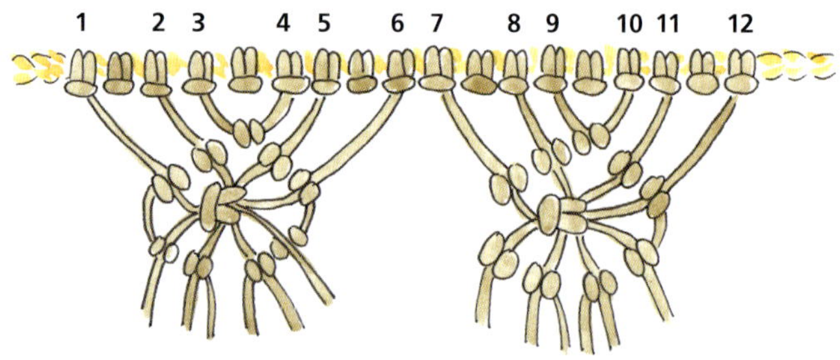

12 Take cord 2 and work a reverse clove hitch knot on cord 4, use cord 5 to work a clove hitch knot on cord 3. Take cord 8 and work a reverse clove hitch knot on cord 10, take cord 11 and work a clove hitch knot on cord 9. Repeat the knotting sequence on each of the other six groups.

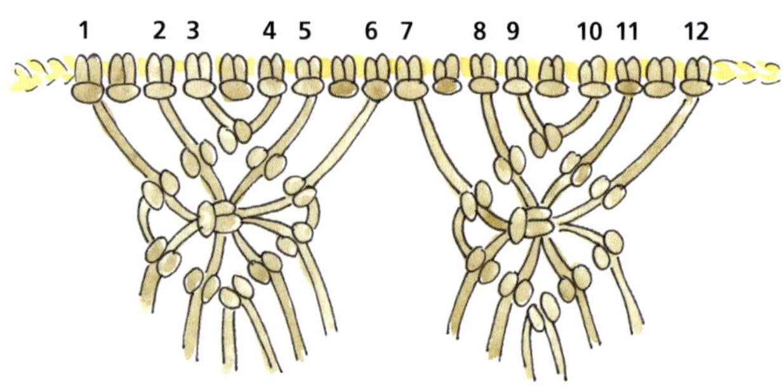

13 Finally, take cord 4 and work a reverse clove hitch knot on cord 3. Take cord 10 and work a clove hitch knot on cord 9. Repeat the knotting sequence on each of the other six groups.

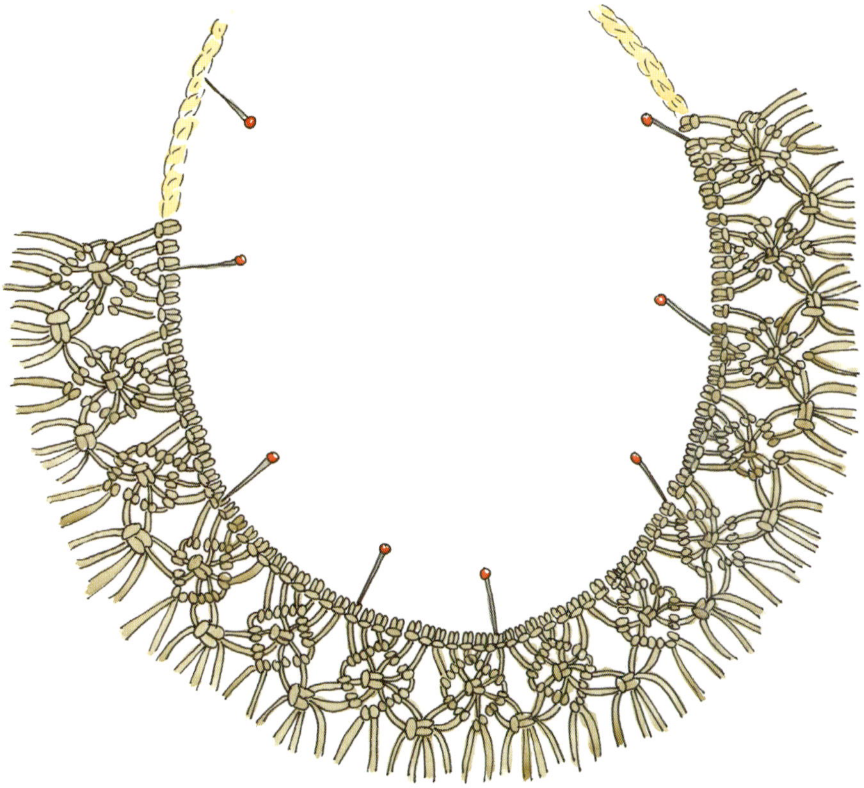

14 Pin the piece to your macramé board in an arc shape. Work a square knot between each circular motif, using cord 12 from the left motif and cord 1 from the right motif as the filler cords, and cord 11 from the left motif and cord 2 from the right motif as the working cords.

15 Repeat steps 8–14 twice more. Then work steps 8–13 once more so there are four rows of circular motifs and three rows of square knots. Trim the ends to ¾in. (2cm).

16 Now make the flowers. Take the mustard yarn and use the crochet hook to make a chain of four stitches (see page 10 for crochet instructions). Join into a circle and work six single crochet (UK: double crochet) into the ring. Join to the first stitch of the round using a slip stitch, trim, and thread the end through the stitch. Join the pink yarn and work one single crochet, one half double crochet, one double crochet, one half double crochet, and one single crochet (UK: one double crochet, one half treble, one treble, one half treble, and one double crochet) into each stitch to create petals. Cut the yarn and thread through the last stitch. Sew in all the ends. Repeat to make another flower.

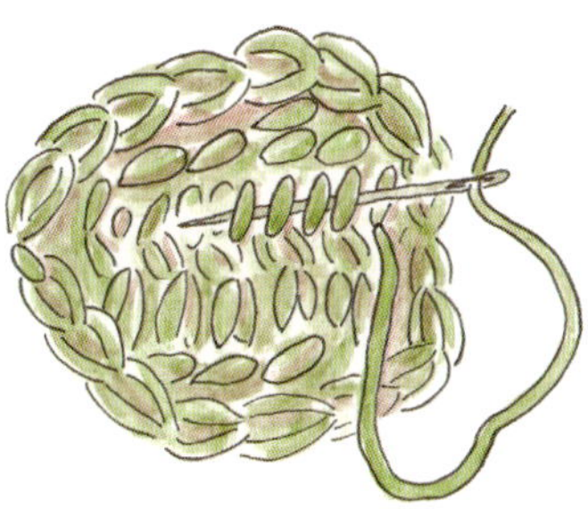

17 To make the leaves, make a chain of seven stitches using the khaki yarn. Then work one single crochet (UK: double crochet) into the first stitch, one half double crochet (UK: half treble) in the next stitch, one double crochet (UK: treble) in each of the next two stitches, and one half double crochet (UK: half treble) in the fifth stitch. Work a chain of three stitches and join to the sixth stitch using a slip stitch. Repeat in reverse on the other side of the chain and then slip stitch into the first stitch to complete. Sew in all the ends. Repeat to make three more leaves.

18 Stitch two leaves to the back of each flower and then sew these to the collar.

CHAPTER 3:

GLITZY AND GLAMOROUS

Knotted earrings

Knot a pair of snazzy earrings with stranded cotton and decorate with sequin and bead tassels and French knots. Once you've mastered the technique, make a pair in every color!

You will need

- Sixteen 14in. (35cm) lengths of purple stranded cotton
- 2 earring findings
- Macramé board and pins
- Four 14in. (35cm) lengths of silver stranded thread
- Two 14in. (35cm) lengths of lime green stranded cotton
- 28 lilac sequins
- 28 green seed beads
- Two 10in. (25cm) lengths of pink stranded cotton
- Needle

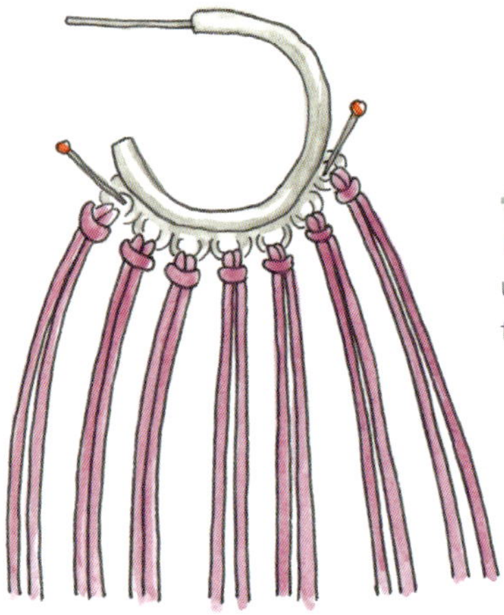

1 Fold seven of the purple threads in half and attach to one of the earring findings using lark's head knots (see page 7). Pin the earring to the macramé board.

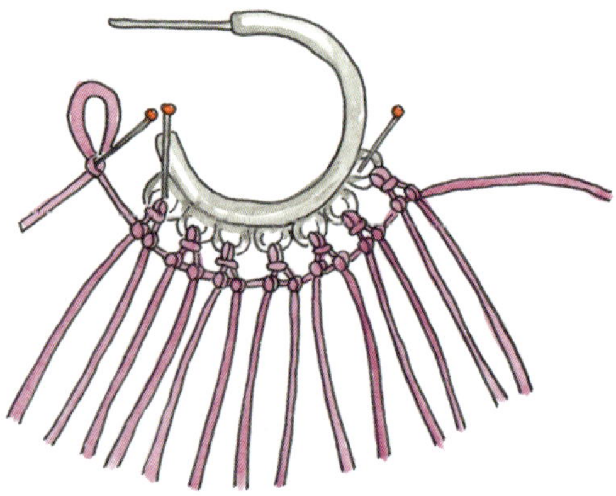

2 Tie a knot in the eighth length of purple thread and pin to the left of the macramé board. This is the filler cord. Work a row of clove hitch knots (see page 8).

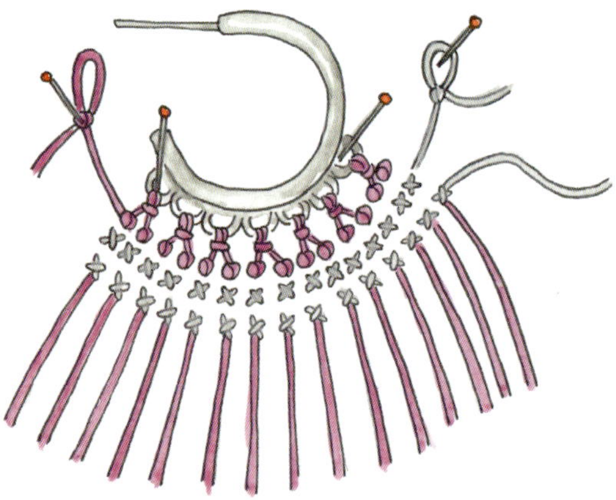

3 Tie a knot in one of the silver lengths and pin to the board on the right side of the earring. Work a row of forward knots (see page 6), including the filler cord so there are 15 knots. Repeat in reverse with backward knots (see page 6) on the next row.

4 **Row 4**: Work a row of reverse clove hitch knots, starting on the right side of the earring.

5 **Rows 5 & 6**: Work a row of backward knots and a row of forward knots in lime green thread, starting on the left side.

6 **Row 7**: Work a row of clove hitch knots starting on the left side.

7 **Rows 8 & 9**: Using another piece of silver thread, work a row of forward knots and a row of backward knots, starting on the right side of the earring.

8 **Row 10**: Work a row of reverse clove hitch knots starting on the right side.

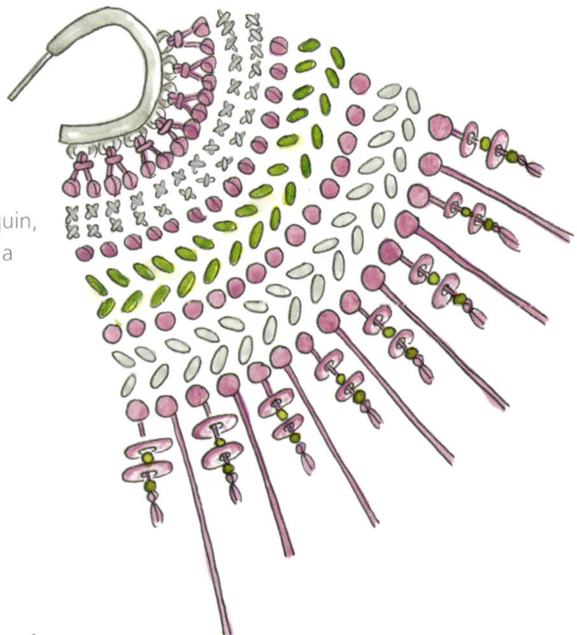

9 To finish, thread a sequin, bead, sequin, bead onto alternate threads and tie a knot to secure. Trim the ends.

10 Sew the remaining threads up the back of the earring and trim.

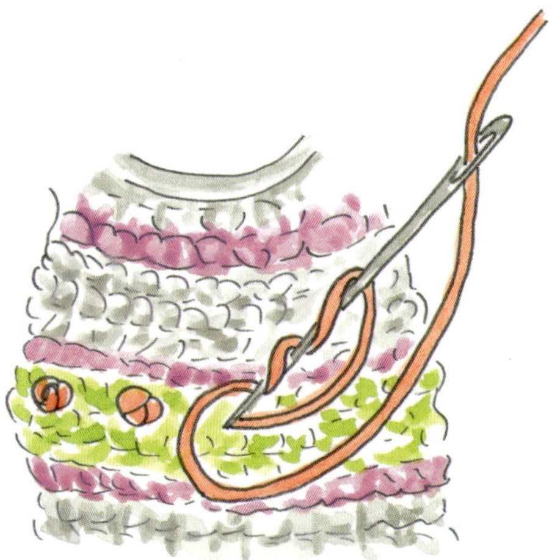

11 Sew four French knots (see page 9) in pink thread along the green stripe.

12 To make the second earring, repeat steps 1–11 but flip the earring finding over and work the knots in reverse (so the first row will be started on the right of the board and be reverse clove hitch knots).

Rose hair tie

Roses are red, Violets are blue, this macramé flower will really stun you! Create a lifelike 3D rose and attach to a hair elastic to make a gorgeous hair accessory.

You will need

- 160yd (146m) of red crochet yarn
- Scissors
- Macramé board and pins
- Needle
- Green felt
- Superglue
- Hair elastic

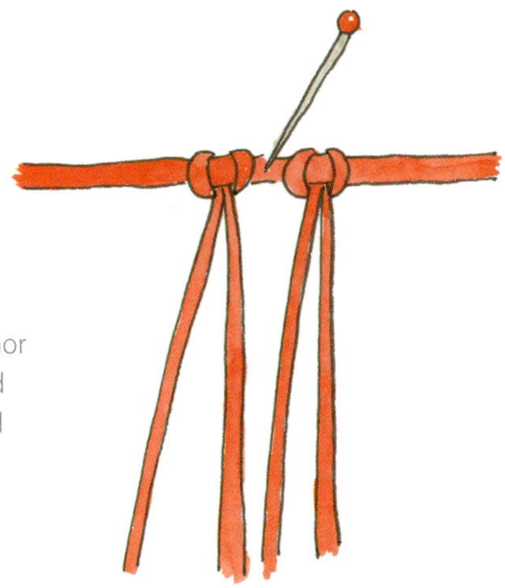

1 Cut 182 lengths of yarn each 32in. (80cm) long. Stretch one across your macramé board and secure as the anchor cord. Fold two other lengths in half and attach to the middle of the anchor cord using lark's head knots (see page 7).

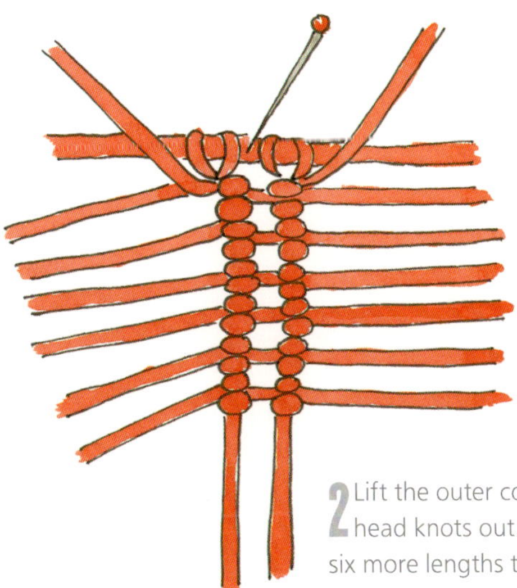

2 Lift the outer cords of the lark's head knots out of the way. Join six more lengths to each inner cord using clove hitch knots (see page 8). The two inner cords are the fillers and the six new cords are the working cords.

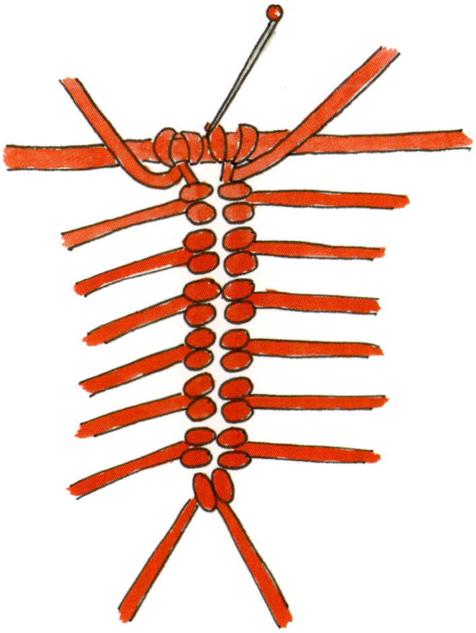

3 Join the two filler cords with a clove hitch knot just below the working cords, using the right-hand cord as the filler and the left-hand cord as the working cord.

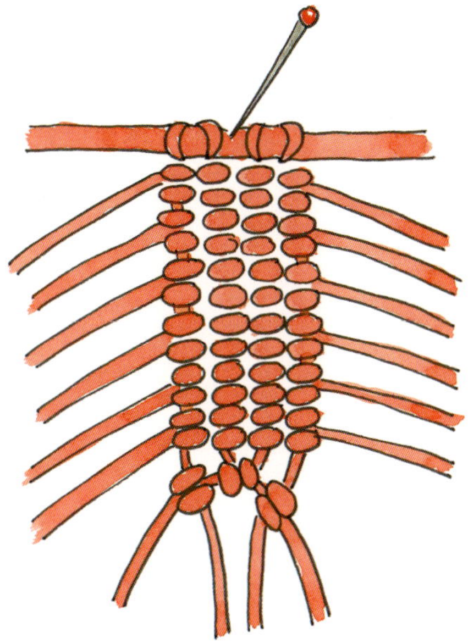

4 Now take the outer cords of the lark's head knots and work another row of clove hitch knots down the six cords on either side, and then on the two filler cords.

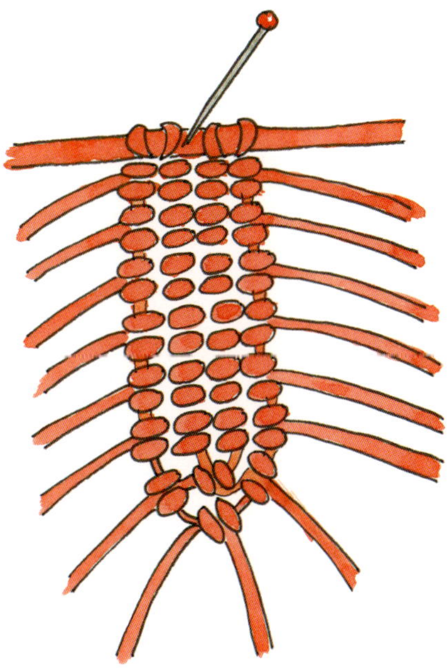

5 Join the bottom center two cords as in step 3.

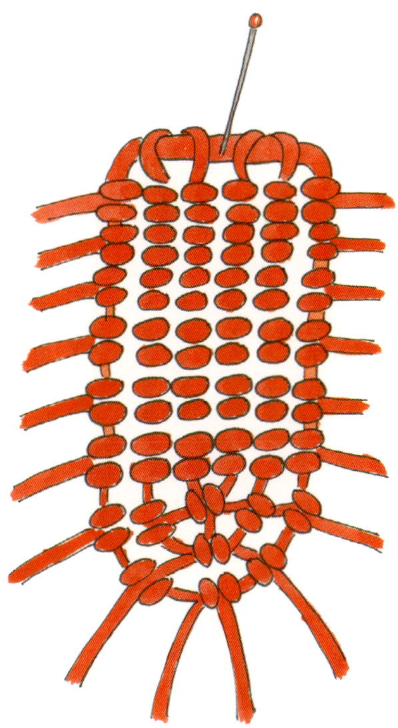

6 Repeat steps 4 and 5 using the ends of the anchor cord, again working down either side and knotting the two center cords at the bottom.

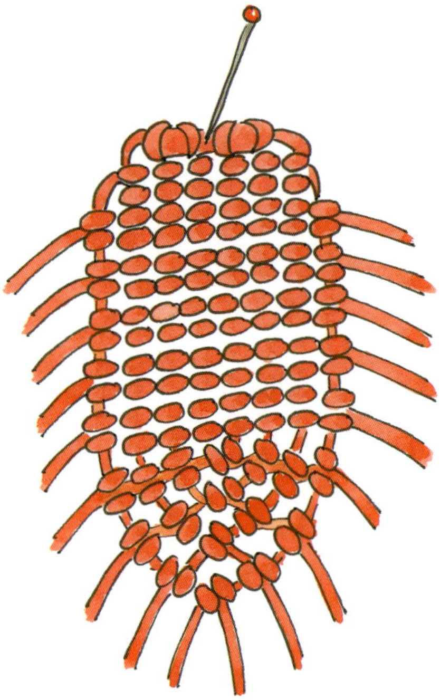

7 Repeat steps 4 and 5 with the top two working cords of the petal to complete. You will have four rows of knots on each side of the petal.

8 Repeat steps 1–7 twice more with a new set of cords, so you have three small petals.

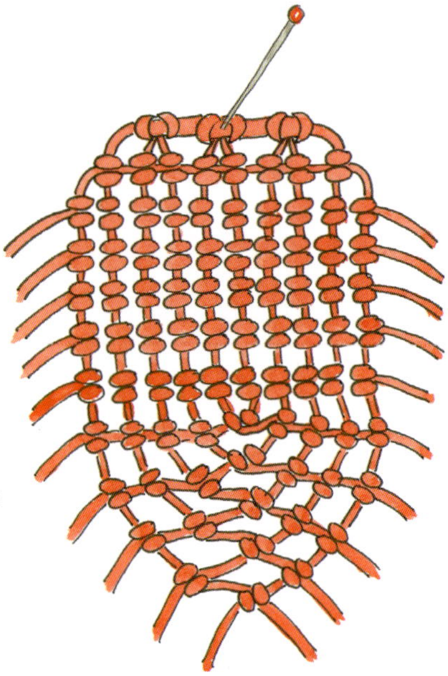

9 Make four medium petals in exactly the same way, but attaching three cords in step 1, so you will finish with five rows of knots on each side of the petal.

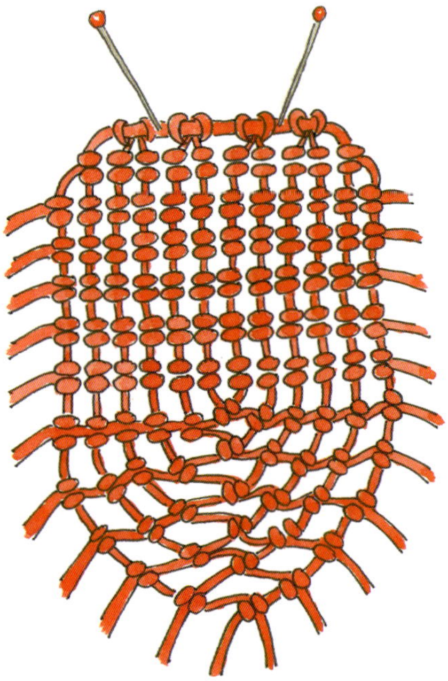

10 Then make five large petals, by attaching four cords in step 1, so you will finish with six rows of knots on each side of the petal.

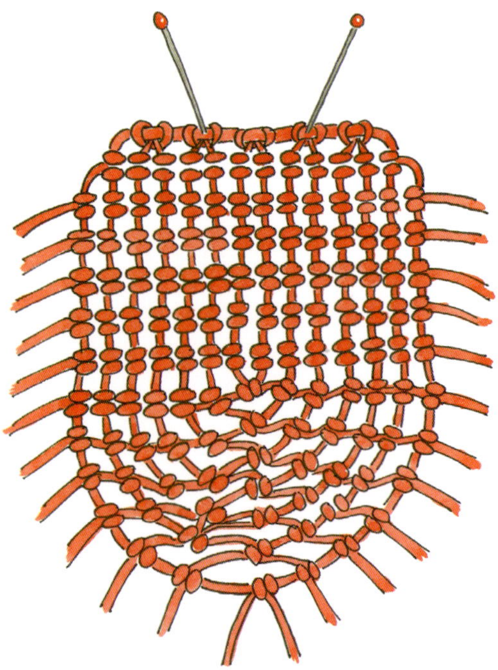

11 Finally, make five extra-large petals with five cords added in step 1, so you will finish with seven rows of knots on each side of the petal.

12 Weave in all the ends, apart from one at the base of one petal in each set of petals—this will be used to sew the flower together.

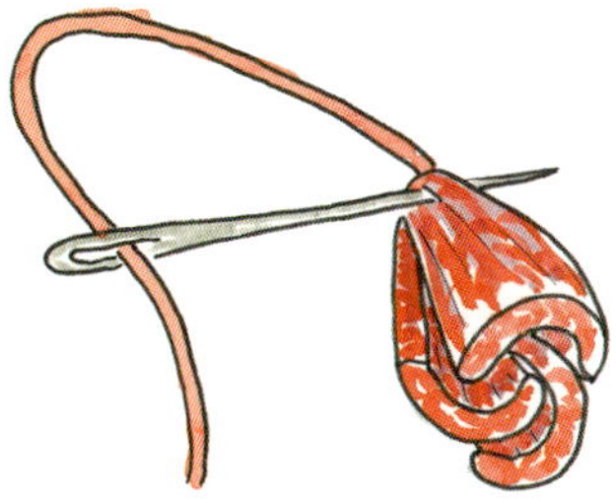

13 Place the three smallest petals together as shown, and use the long end to sew them together to create a tight core.

14 Sew the four medium petals around the core, then the five large, and finally the five extra-large petals to create a perfect rose shape.

15 Cut a piece of green felt to look like two leaves—I used pinking shears to give a crinkled effect. Stick the hair elastic to the back of the flower using superglue and hide the join with the felt leaves. Allow to dry completely before using.

Beaded cross necklace

Use bold metallic beads and threads to make this gorgeous cross pendant necklace.

You will need

- Two 40in. (100cm) lengths of copper metallic beading cord
- Leather cord necklace
- Macramé board and pins
- 14 metallic beads
- Four 30in. (75cm) lengths of copper metallic beading cord
- Scissors
- Glue

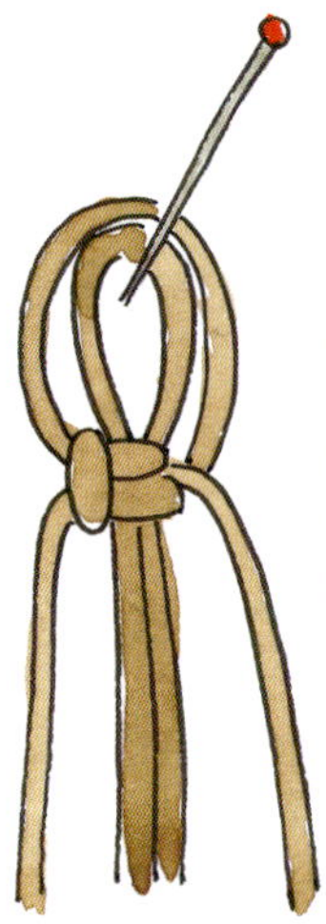

1 Fold both the longer cords in half and work a square knot (see page 7), leaving a loop at the top long enough so that your leather cord will fit through it. Pin to your macramé board.

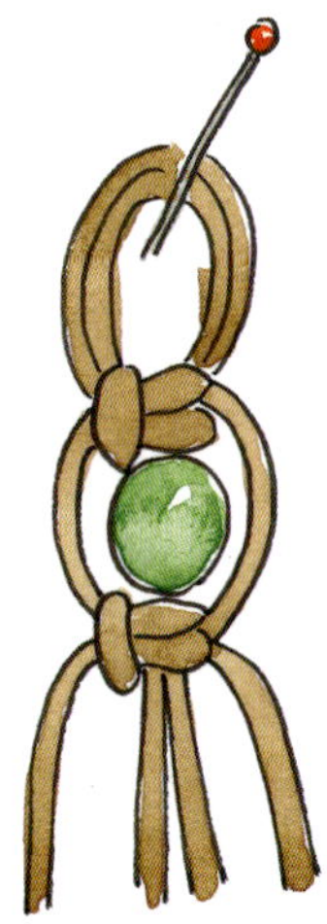

2 Thread a bead onto both of the central filler cords and work another square knot underneath to secure it.

3 Repeat step 2 twice more to create the top of your cross.

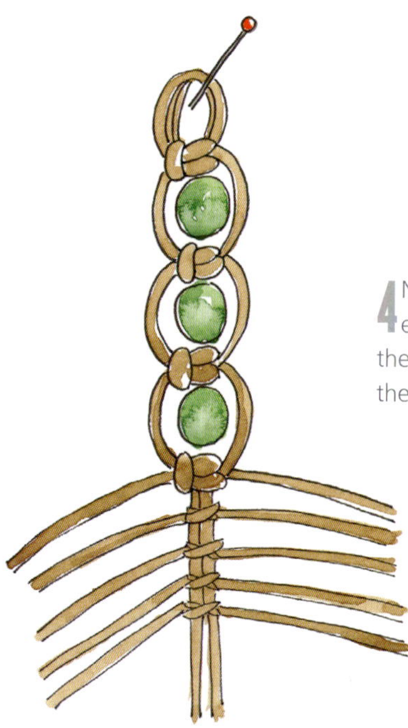

4 Now take the two working cords on either edge out to the side, out of the way. Tie the four shorter cords to your filler cords, so there are equal lengths of cord on each side.

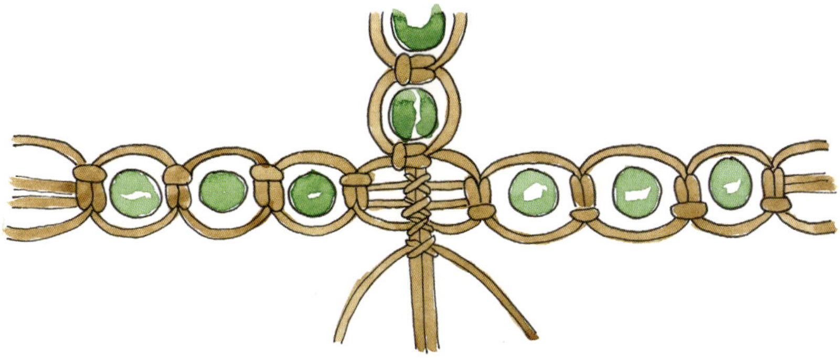

5 Now work the sides of the cross. Take the four cords on one side and repeat steps 2 and 3, starting with a square knot. Repeat on the other side.

6 Go back to the four central cords and repeat step 2 five times downward, so there are five beads.

7 Dab a spot of glue at the back of each of the knots at the end of a line. Once dry, trim the cords close to the knot.

8 Thread the necklace onto the leather cord to complete.

Beaded wave bracelet

A heavily beaded bracelet in a rich color palette—this type of detailed knotting is called micro macramé.

You will need

- Six 40in. (100cm) lengths of 0.1mm mustard nylon beading cord
- 71 matte turquoise seed beads
- 65 copper faceted seed beads
- 70 cream seed beads
- 65 turquoise faceted seed beads
- 7 turquoise 5mm faceted beads
- 71 matte copper seed beads
- Macramé board and pins
- Scissors
- Lighter

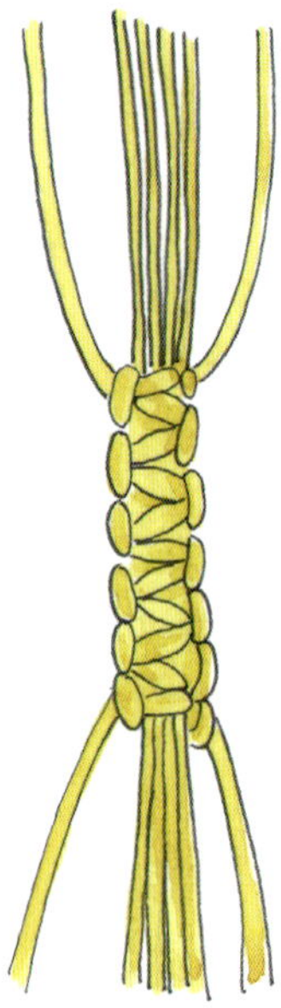

1 Pin the six cords to the macramé board and bunch together in the middle of their length. With the four center cords as the filler cords, use the two outer cords to work a 1in. (2.5cm) sequence of square knots (see page 7) in the middle of the lengths.

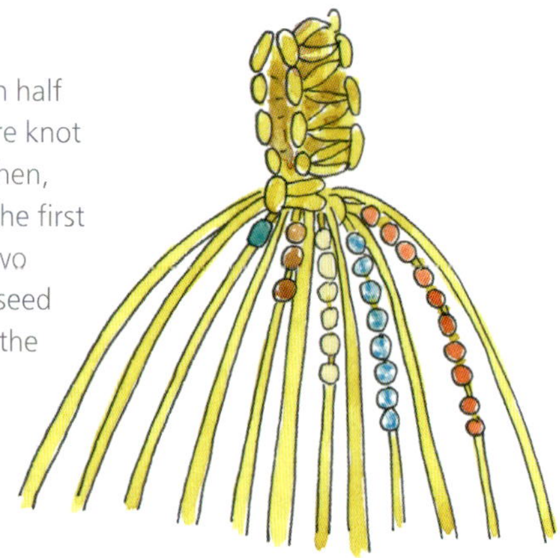

2 Fold the length of knots in half and work one more square knot to hold the loop together. Then, working from the left, add the first set of beads: skip the first two cords, one matte turquoise seed bead on the next cord, skip the fourth cord, three copper faceted beads on the next cord, skip the sixth cord, five cream beads on the next cord, skip the eighth cord, eight turquoise faceted beads on the next cord, skip the tenth cord, ten matte copper beads on the next cord, skip the 12th cord.

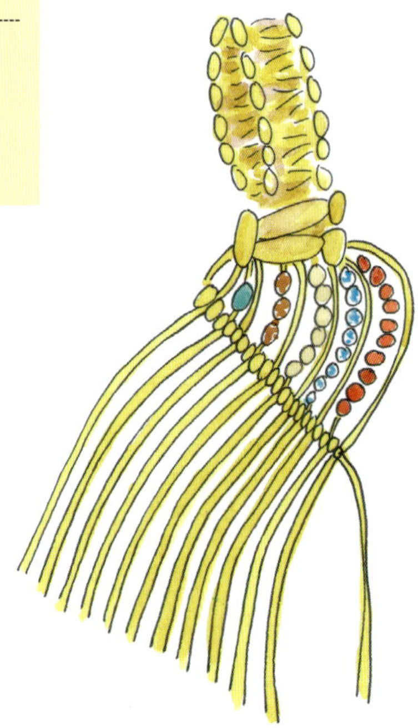

3 Starting from the left side, and using the first cord as the working cord, work a clove hitch knot (see page 8) on each of the 11 cords.

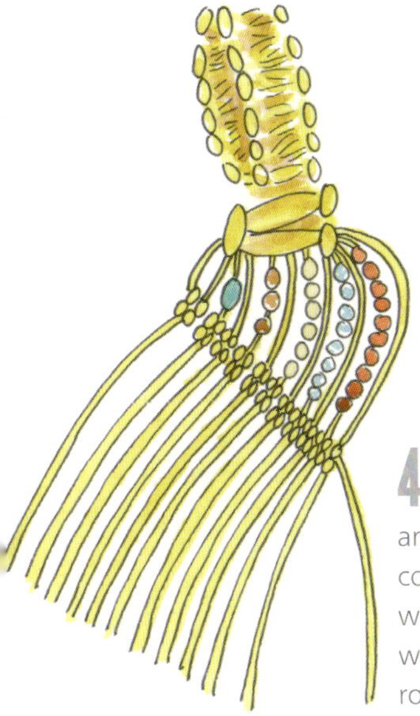

4 Again starting from the left and using the first cord as the working cord, work a second row of clove hitch knots across all the cords.

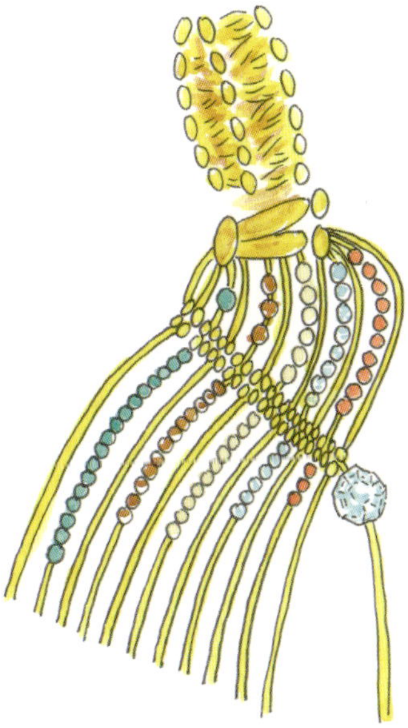

5 Now work the first wave of beads. Starting from the left side, thread the following onto the cords: skip the first cord, 17 turquoise seed beads on the next cord, skip the third cord, 12 copper faceted beads on the next cord, skip the fifth cord, ten cream beads on the next cord, skip the seventh cord, six faceted turquoise beads on the next cord, skip the ninth cord, three matte copper beads on the next cord, skip the 11th cord, one large turquoise faceted bead on the final cord.

6 Starting from the right side, and using the first cord as the working cord, work a row of reverse clove hitch knots (see page 8). Repeat with the next cord to make a second row of reverse clove hitch knots from right to left.

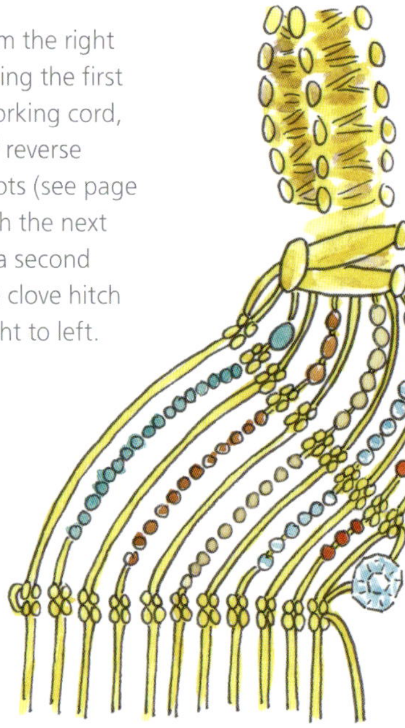

7 Work the second wave of beads. Starting from the right side, thread the following onto the threads: skip the first cord, 17 matte copper beads on the next cord, skip the third cord, 12 faceted turquoise beads on the next cord, skip the fifth cord, ten cream beads on the next cord, skip the seventh cord, six faceted copper beads on the next cord, skip the ninth cord, three matte turquoise beads on the next cord, skip the 11th cord, one large turquoise faceted bead on the final cord. Starting from the left side each time, work two rows of clove hitch knots.

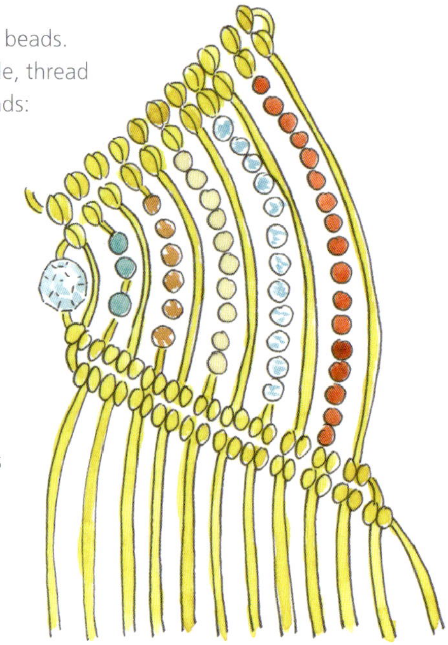

8 Repeat steps 5–7 twice more.

9 For the final half wave of the bracelet, skip the first cord, ten matte turquoise beads on the next cord, skip the third cord, eight copper faceted beads on the next cord, skip the fifth cord, six cream beads on the next cord, skip the seventh cord, three turquoise faceted beads on the next cord, skip the ninth cord, one matte copper bead on the next cord, skip the 11th cord, one large turquoise faceted bead on the final cord. Starting from the right side each time, work two rows of clove hitch knots. Divide the 12 threads into three equal bunches and braid for 3in. (7.5cm). Make a knot to fit into the loop at the other end, then trim and seal the ends with the lighter to secure.

Flower brooch

This project is worked in a circular way, unlike most of the others in this book. I added a variety of beads and metal nuts to the brooch—it would look fab pinned to a denim jacket or shopper.

You will need

- Twenty-four 40in. (100cm) lengths of pale pink cotton yarn
- ½in. (12mm) split ring
- 12 brass nuts
- 48 green seed beads
- 48 blue seed beads
- 12 yellow seed beads
- Glue
- Badge pin
- Needle and thread

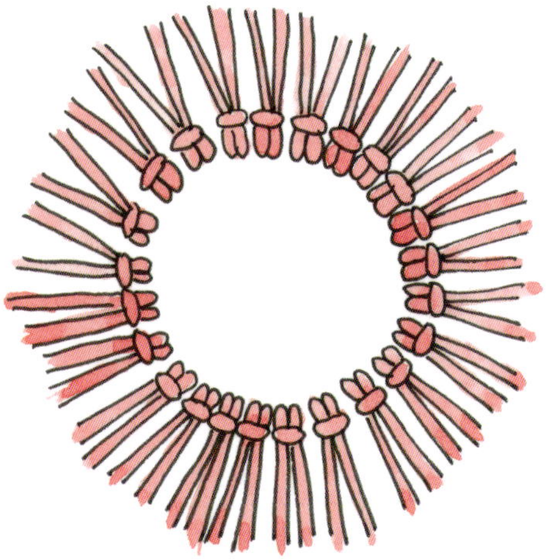

1 Fold each of the 24 threads in half and attach them around the split ring using lark's head knots (see page 7).

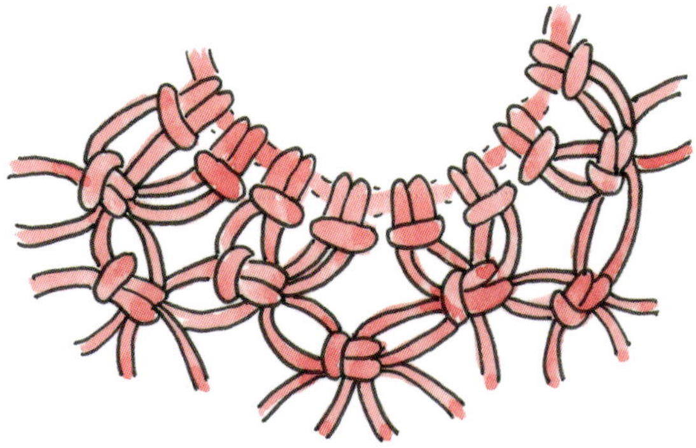

2 Work two rounds of alternating square knots (see page 8).

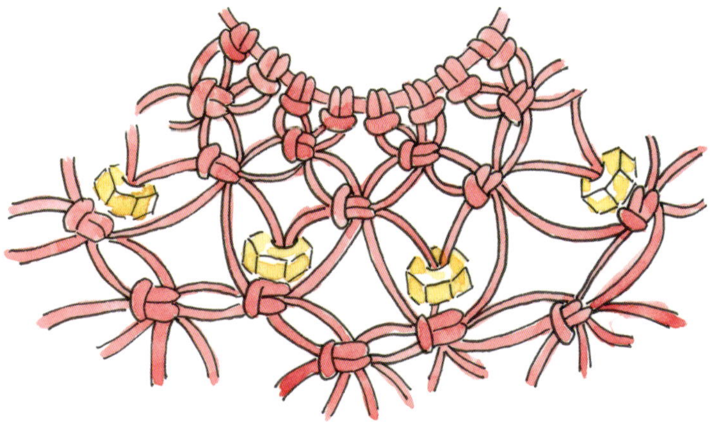

3 On the third round, take the outer working cords from two adjacent knots and thread on a brass nut. Tie a square knot as normal below the nut. Repeat all round.

4 Work another round of alternating square knots.

5 Thread two green seed beads onto both central filler cords of each square knot, then work a round of alternating square knots beneath as normal. Work a second round of alternating square knots.

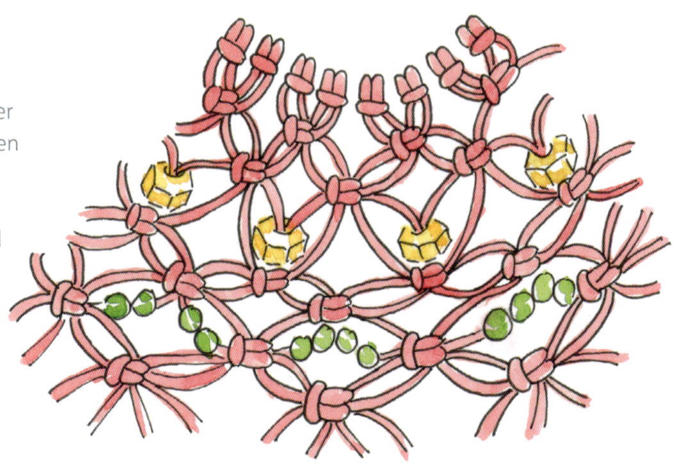

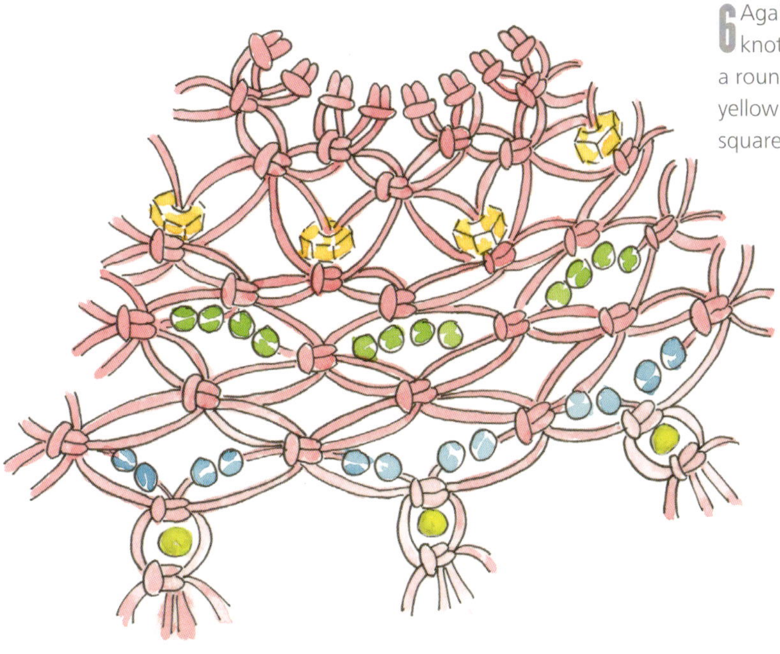

6 Again, take the outer working cords from two adjacent knots and thread two blue seed beads onto each. Work a round of alternating square knots. Finally, add a single yellow bead to each pair of filler cords, before tying a final square knot.

7 Add a dab of glue to the back of the last knots to secure. Allow to dry and then trim the ends.

8 Sew the badge pin to the back of the flower to complete.

Butterfly Hairclip

This beaded butterfly hairclip would be great for a wedding or special occasion, instead of a fascinator. Use floss colors that match your outfit—or in the colors of a real butterfly, if you prefer.

You will need

- Three 60in. (150cm) lengths of black stranded embroidery floss
- Four 30in. (75cm) lengths of black stranded embroidery floss
- Ten 30in. (75cm) lengths of bright pink stranded embroidery floss
- Eight 30in. (75cm) lengths of cream stranded embroidery floss
- Twelve 30in. (75cm) lengths of turquoise stranded embroidery floss
- Two 30in. (75cm) lengths of green stranded embroidery floss
- 10 turquoise beads
- Sewing needle
- Two 24in. (60cm) lengths of black stranded embroidery floss
- 4in. (10cm) length of black stranded embroidery floss
- Kirby grip
- Macramé board and pins

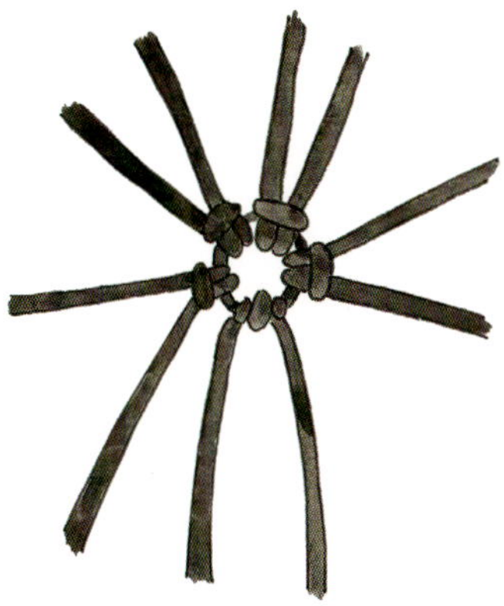

1 To begin, you will need one piece of black embroidery floss 60in. (150cm) long and four pieces 30in. (75cm) long. Attach the four shorter lengths to the longer one using lark's head knots (see page 7), then tie the ends of the longer piece into a circle using a forward knot (see page 6). Arrange as shown.

2 Start by making the two right wings. Each length of floss is one cord in the instructions.
Row 1: Take the right-hand end of the long black cord forming the circle (this is your working cord) and work a forward knot on the next black cord to the right, then attach a pink cord to the working cord using a lark's head knot, work a forward knot on each of the next two black cords, attach a second pink cord on the working cord, and finish with a forward knot on the fourth cord.

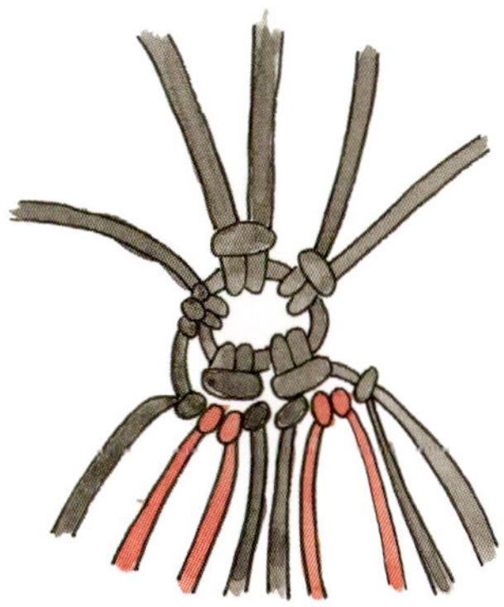

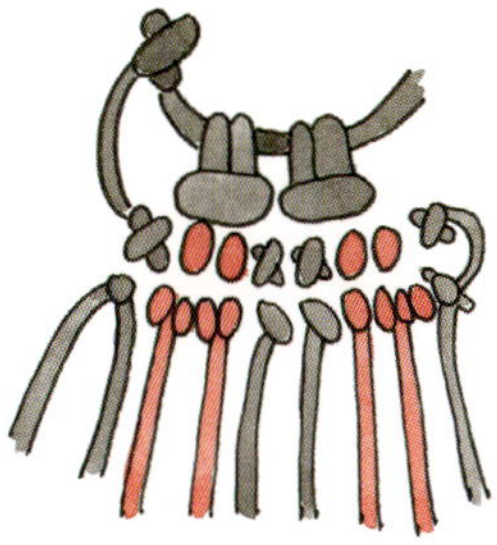

3 **Row 2**: Work back over the same cords, using backward knots (see page 6) on the black cords and reverse clove hitch knots (see page 8) on the pink cords.

4 **Row 3**: Now work as row 1 again, but this time attach a cream cord to the working cord between each pair of pink strands on both wings.

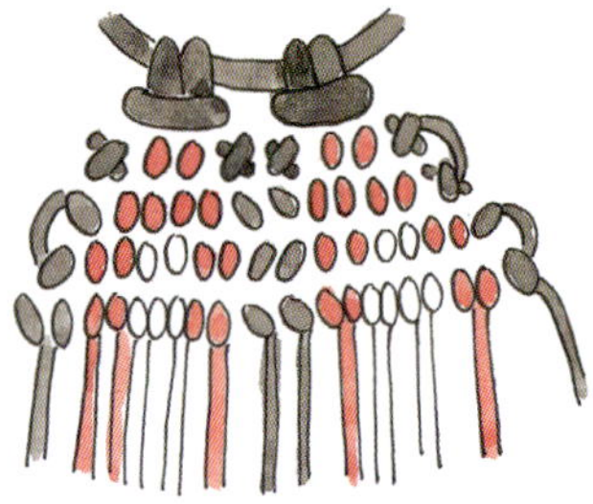

5 **Row 4**: Work back the other way as in step 3, using backward knots on the black cords and reverse clove hitch knots on the pink and cream cords.

6 **Row 5**: Using a lark's head knot, add a pink cord in the center of one wing and another cream one to the center of the other wing.

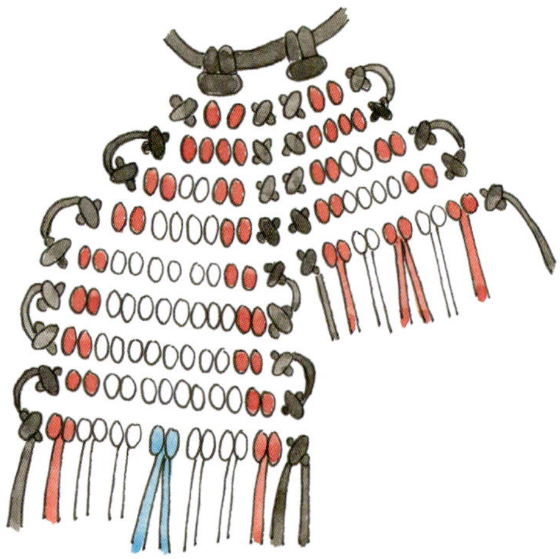

7 **Rows 6–8**: Now start working on the small wing only—this will be the left wing in the way you are working. Work three more rows, not adding any extra cords.
Row 9: Use a lark's head knot to add a turquoise cord in the center of the wing.

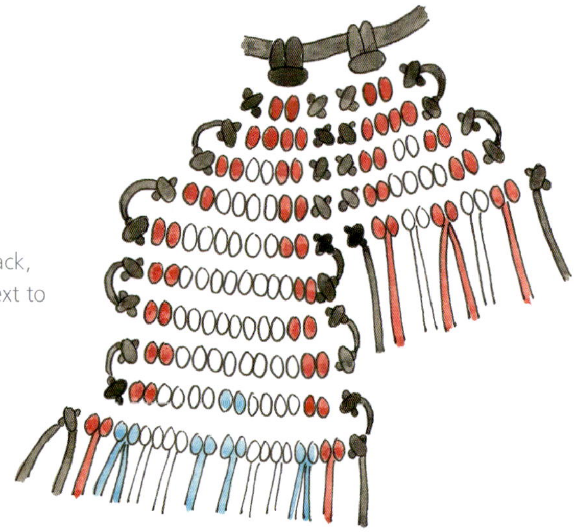

8 **Row 10**: On the way back, add a turquoise cord next to each pink cord.

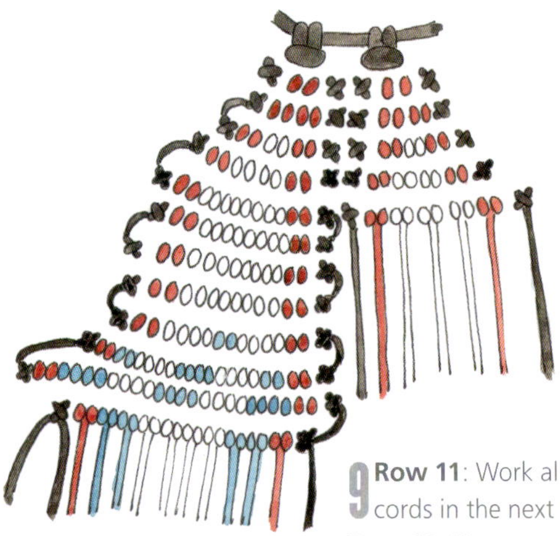

9 **Row 11**: Work all the cords in the next row.
Row 12: Now start reducing the cords. Skip the two central turquoise cords in the next row.

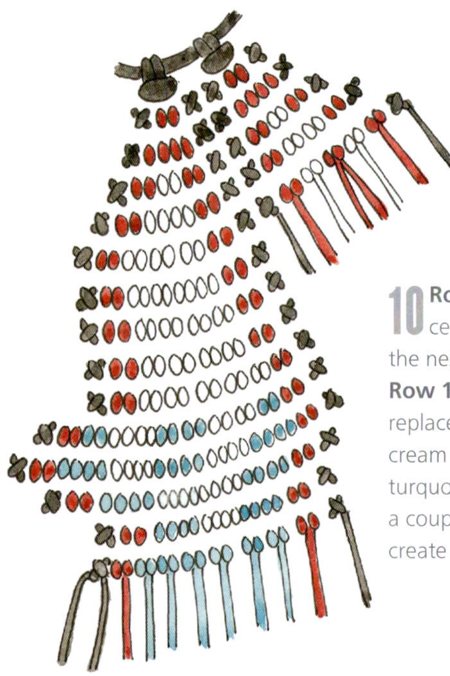

10 **Row 13**: Skip the two central cream cords in the next row.
Row 14: In the next row, replace the remaining two cream cords with the two turquoise cords you dropped a couple of rows earlier, to create a solid turquoise row.

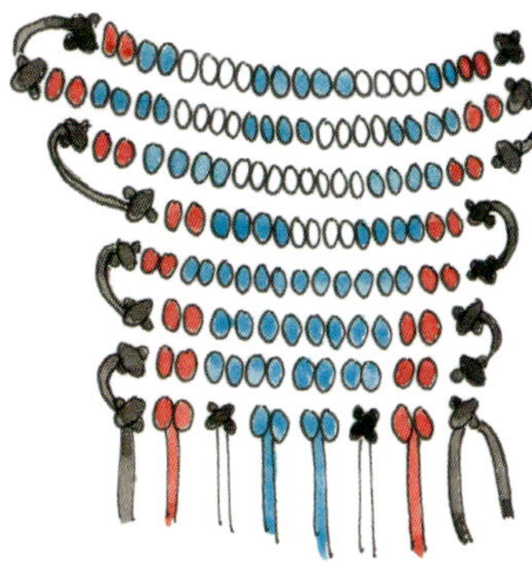

11 **Row 15**: Drop the central two cords.
Row 16: Work all of the next row.
Row 17: Work forward knots on the outer turquoise cords to create black dots.

12 **Row 18**: Work backward knots on all the cords so that the row is all black, apart from the two pink dots near each end.
Row 19: Work all forward knots, skipping the pink cords.
Row 20: Work all backward knots on the next row.
Row 21: Work all forward knots on the next row, but skip the central two cords.
Row 22: Work all backward knots.
Row 23: Work all forward knots on the next row, but skip the central two cords.
Row 24: Finally, knot the last two cords together to complete the wing.

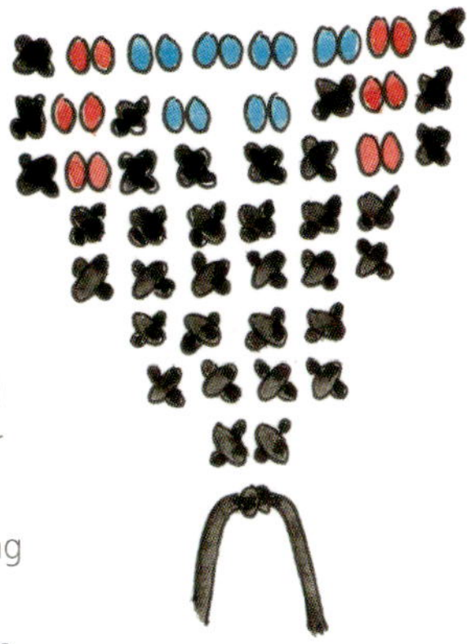

13 Sew all the ends in to complete. Sew a bead at the tip of the wing.

14 Now go back to finish the larger wing.
Row 6: Use a lark's head knot to add another 60in. (150cm) black working cord to the left of the wing. Work a forward knot on the outer black cords, add a green cord in the central position and work clove hitch knots on the colored cords.
Row 7: Add a pink cord in the central position. Work reverse clove hitch knots on the rest of the row.
Row 8: Add a cream cord in the central position. Work clove hitch knots on the rest of the row.
Row 9: Add a turquoise cord in the central position. Work reverse clove hitch knots on the rest of the row.
Row 10: Work clove hitch knots on the whole row.
Row 11: Add a pink cord in the central position. Work reverse clove hitch knots on the rest of the row.
Row 12: Work clove hitch knots on the whole row.
Row 13: Add a turquoise cord between the first cream and second pink cord on both sides of the wing. Work reverse clove hitch knots on the rest of the row.
Row 14: Work a row of clove hitch knots.

15 **Row 15**: Work reverse clove hitch knots, skipping the central two pink cords to start reducing the wing size.

Row 16: Work every other cord with a forward knot to create black dots; the colored knots should be clove hitch knots.

Row 17: Work every other cord (the alternate cords to row 16) with a backward knot using the black cord. Skipping the two center turquoise cords, all the other knots should be reverse clove hitch knots.

Row 18: Work two cords of each three with forward knots; the others should be clove hitch knots.

Row 19: Work a row of all backward knots, using the black cord.

Rows 20–33: Keep working rows of forward and backward knots, skipping two cords in each row. You may want to do a plain row without any reductions every third row so it doesn't get too tight.

16 Repeat steps 2–15 to make the second half of the butterfly, this time beginning by working to the left with the left cord end from the circle.

17 Sew four beads onto the black part of the large wings. Sew in all the ends to neaten.

18 To make the body, attach the two 24in. (60cm) cords to the bottom of the original circle between the wings, using a lark's head knot, and then work square knots (see page 7) for 1¼in. (3cm). Tie a knot and trim.

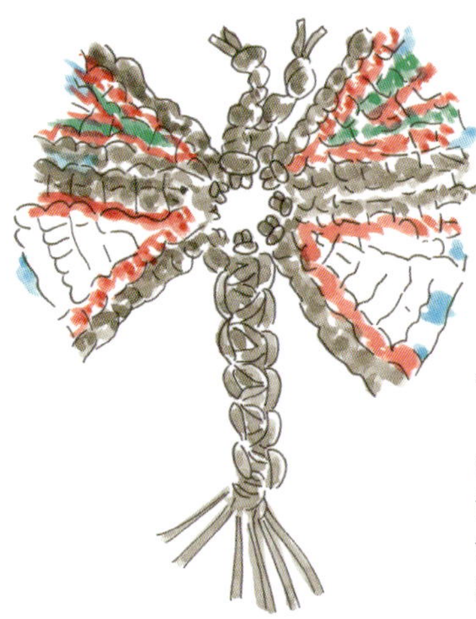

19 To make the antennae, attach the 4in. (10cm) piece of black embroidery floss on the opposite side to the body using a lark's head knot, and trim to the length you want. To complete your clip, sew a Kirby grip to the back of the butterfly.

Circular earrings

These striking earrings look fabulous! They have a retro 1980s look to them that I really love.

You will need

- Twelve 48in. (120cm) lengths of cotton thread in each of mustard, gray, orange, and green
- Macramé board and pins
- Two 80in. (200cm) lengths of thick string
- 24 triangular metal beads
- Needle
- Earring findings
- Scissors

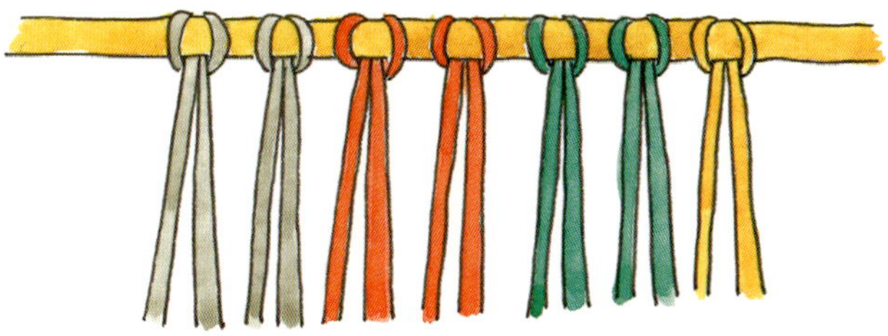

1 Pin one of the mustard threads to the macramé board as an anchor thread. Fold two gray, two orange, two green, and one mustard threads in half and attach to the anchor thread using lark's head knots (see page 7).

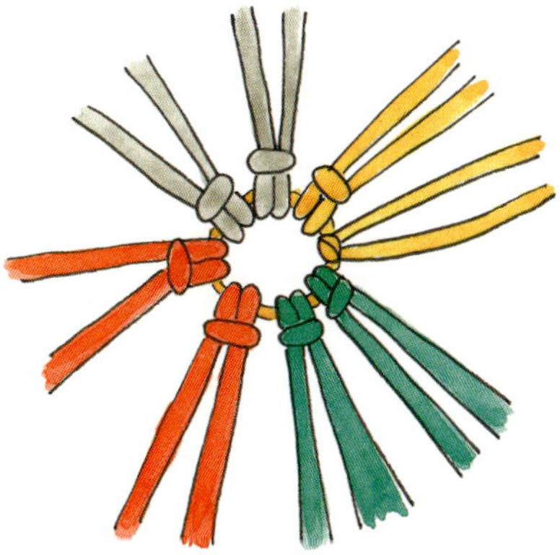

2 Release the anchor thread and tie the two ends together to form a circle.

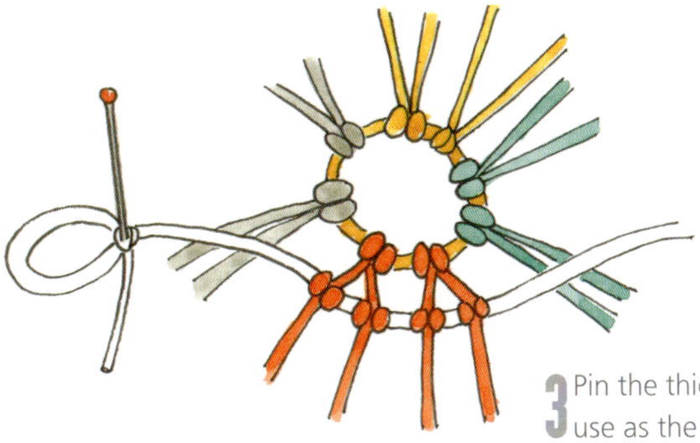

3 Pin the thick string to the macramé board to use as the filler cord. Working from left to right, make four clove hitch knots (see page 8) over the filler cord using the orange threads. Repeat all around the circle, working the clove hitch knots with each color of thread in turn.

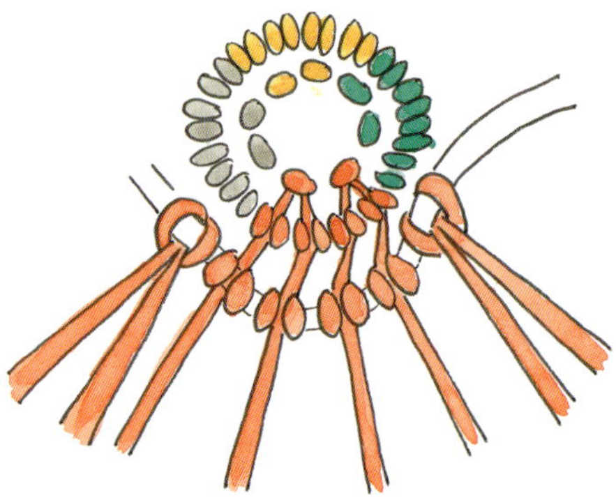

4 **Row 2**: Take another orange thread and fold it in half, then attach it to the filler cord on the left of the orange section using a lark's head knot. Work clove hitch knots with the four orange threads, then fold another orange thread in half and attach to the filler cord on the other side using a lark's head knot. Repeat with each colored section to add an extra thread to the start and end of each section.

5 **Row 3**: Use the orange threads to work clove eight hitch knots on the filler cord. Repeat with the other color threads all round.

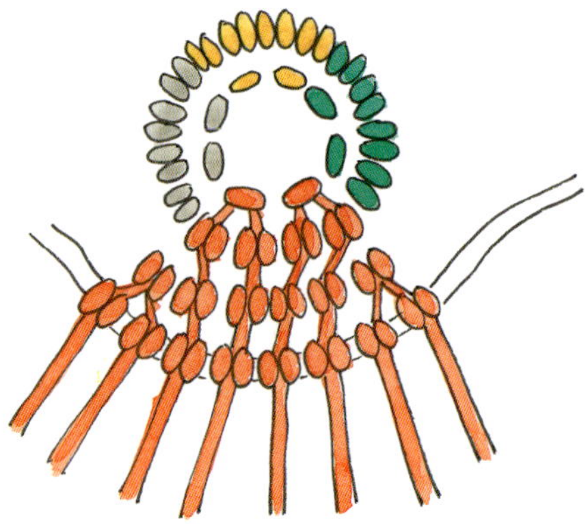

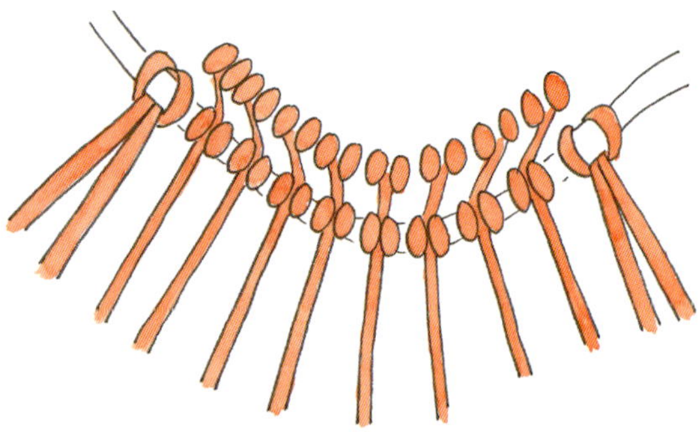

6 **Row 4**: Take another orange thread and fold it in half, then attach it to the filler cord on the left of the orange section using a lark's head knot. Work clove hitch knots with the eight orange threads, then fold another orange thread in half and attach to the filler cord on the other side using a lark's head knot. Repeat with each colored section to add an extra thread to the start and end of each section.

7 When you have completed row 4 on the gray section, start working backward and forward on this section only in straight rows, dropping a thread at both ends of each row to make the triangular shape. Continue until you have four working cords left at the top of the triangle.

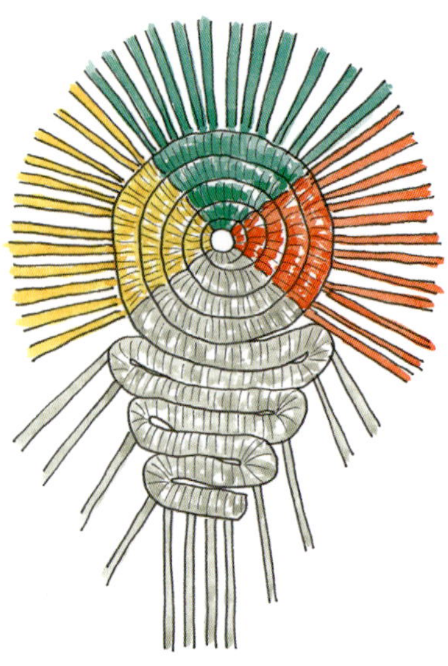

8 Use the ends of some of the working cords to attach triangular beads evenly around the outer edge of the earring. Thread the ends up through the knots and trim off neatly. Sew an earring finding at the top of the earring.

9 Sew in all the remaining thread ends and trim to secure.

10 Repeat steps 1–10 to make a second earring.

Sequin headband

Combine crochet with braiding and sequins to create this glamorous headband piece. It would look great for a night out, wedding, or festival.

You will need

- ⅞oz (25g) of gray yarn
- Approx. 150 sequins in each of gold, navy, and purple
- 4mm crochet hook
- 1¼ x 1½in. (3 x 4cm) piece of gray felt
- Scissors
- Superglue or sewing thread and needle

1 Thread approximately 150 purple sequins onto the gray yarn.

2 Make a slip knot with the yarn and insert the crochet hook. Make a chain of five stitches (see page 10).

3 Continue crocheting a chain, but before you make each stitch push a sequin up to the hook and then secure it in place with the stitch.

4 Continue until the cord is approximately 22in. (55cm) long. Make a chain of five stitches at the end and then thread the yarn end through the last stitch to secure.

5 Repeat steps 1–5 with the navy and the gold sequins.

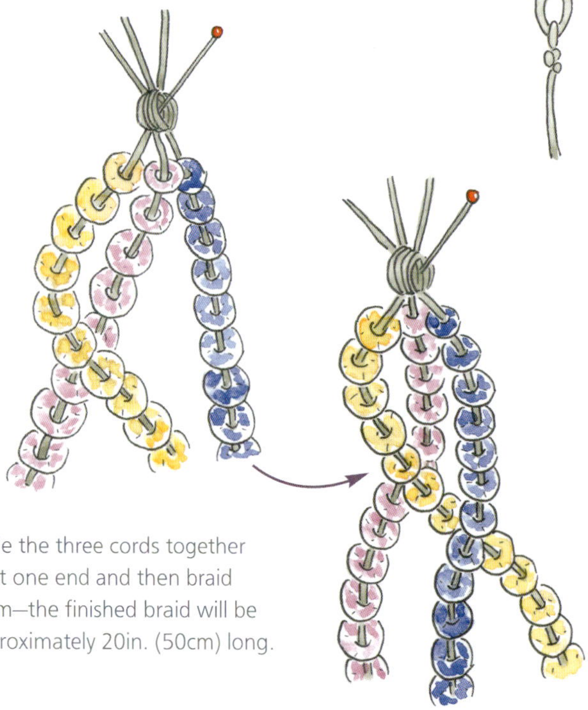

6 Tie the three cords together at one end and then braid them—the finished braid will be approximately 20in. (50cm) long.

7 Tie the two ends of the braid together and then cover the join with the piece of felt, by wrapping it around and holding it in place with superglue or a few stitches.

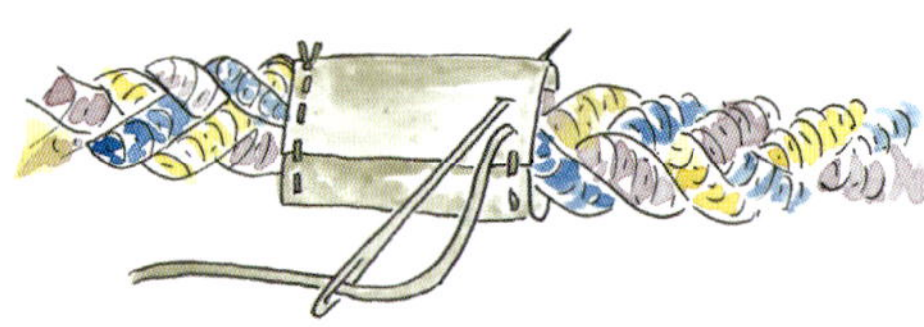

CHAPTER 4:

CHIC AND CONTEMPORARY

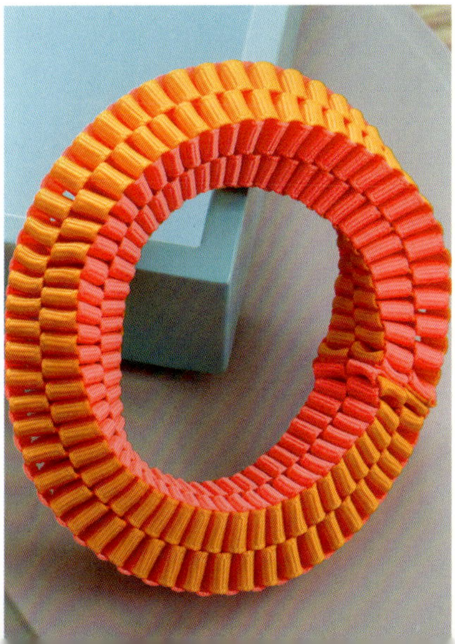

Alternating lark's head knot necklace

Combine nylon cord, silky cord, and beads to create this fashionable necklace that will add a touch of style to any outfit.

1 Pin the chain to the macramé board and then lay the thick mustard string along the central section for approximately 9in. (22.5cm).

2 Tie one piece of olive green nylon cord around the chain and thick string at one end of the section where they meet, so that you have two cord ends the same length on each side.

3 Work alternating lark's head knots (see page 7) along the length of chain and thick string. Thread the ends up through the knots and trim to finish the first row.

You will need

- Gold chain
- Macramé board and pins
- 40in. (1m) length of thick mustard string
- 35 square metal gold beads
- Two 200in. (5m) lengths of 0.5mm olive green nylon cord
- Two 200in. (5m) lengths of 0.2mm mustard silky cord
- Two 200in. (5m) lengths of 0.2mm khaki silky cord

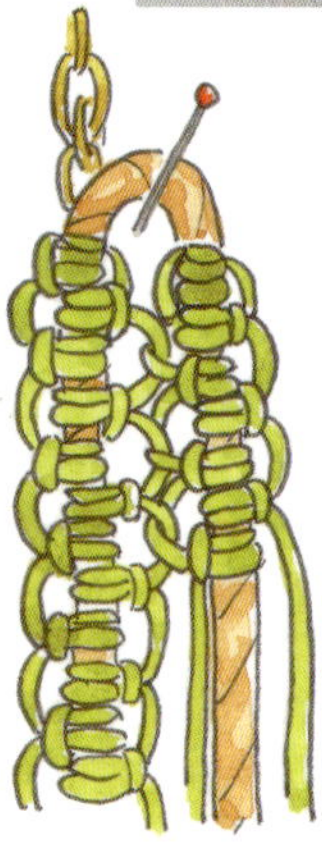

4 Bend the thick string round and pin in place. Knot the next piece of olive green nylon cord to the string and start working more alternating lark's head knots, but this time thread the left cord through the right loops of the first row before tying each knot to join the rows together.

5 On the third row, bend the string around as before, and then tie a piece of mustard cord to the string. Work alternating larks's head knots, this time threading the right-hand cord through the loops on row 2 before tying them. As this cord is thicker, you may need to skip the odd loop to even out the knots.

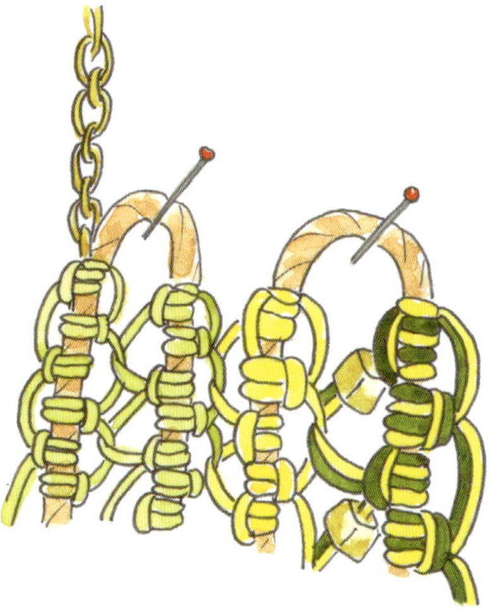

6 For the final row, join one mustard and one khaki silky cord together and tie to the string. Work the alternating cords as in step 4, but thread a bead onto one of the left cords as you thread them through row 3.

7 To complete the necklace, thread the string ends up through the second and third rows.

Beaded 4-ply cord bracelet

Braid a delicate bracelet with seed bead detail—try using thicker cords and bigger beads for a more dramatic effect.

1 Place the two cords together and thread the large cream bead to the center. Tie a knot to hold the bead in place.

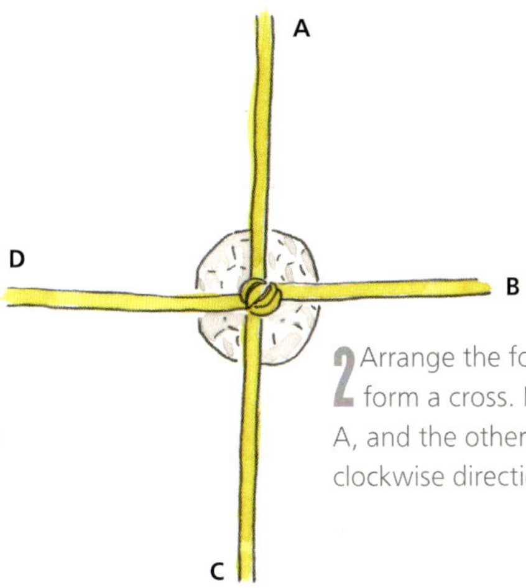

2 Arrange the four cord ends to form a cross. Note the top cord as A, and the others B, C, and D in a clockwise direction, as shown.

3 Take cord A and bring it round and down over cord B.

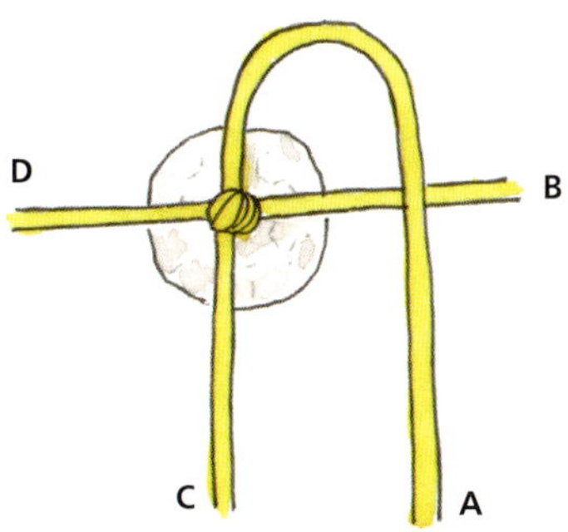

You will need

Mustard bracelet

- Two 200cm (5m) lengths of 0.5mm mustard nylon cord
- Large round cream bead
- Cream seed beads
- Scissors and lighter

Green bracelet

- Four 200cm (5m) lengths of 0.5mm green nylon cord
- Large round amber bead
- Amber seed beads
- Scissors and lighter

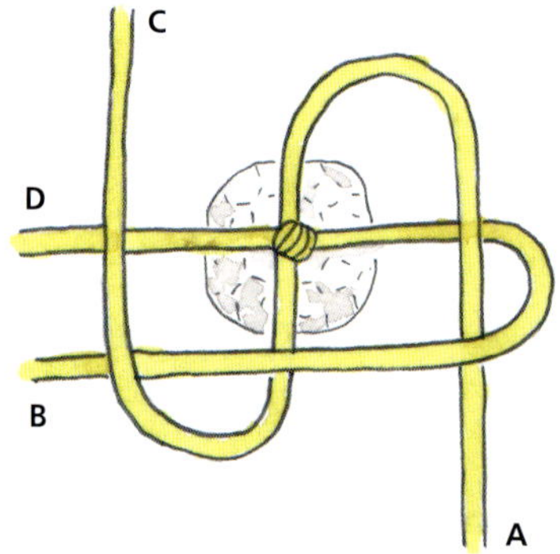

4 Take cord B round and to the right over cords A and C. Take cord C round and up over cord D.

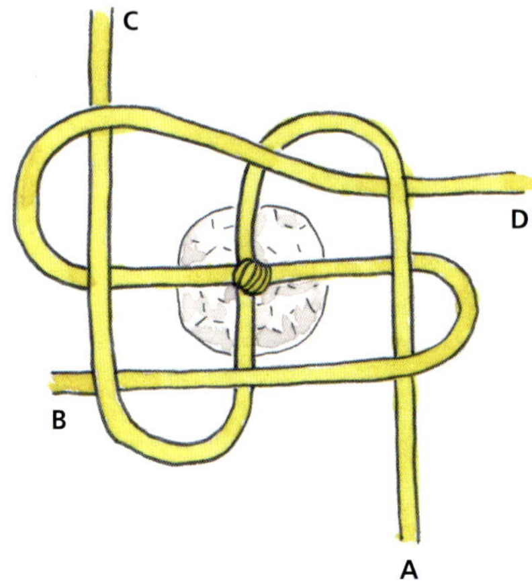

5 Finally, take cord D over cord C and thread through the loop formed by cord A.

6 Pull the cords gently and evenly to create a knot.

7 Repeat this knot, always starting from the top cord, for 2in. (5cm). Then, for the next 2in. (5cm) of knotting, add a seed bead to each cord before knotting.

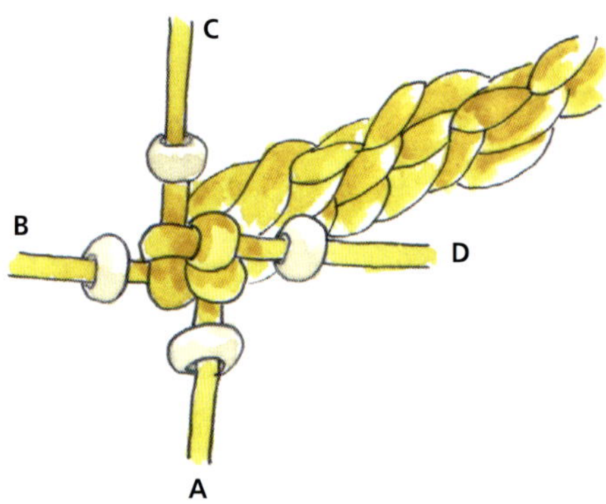

8 Work plain knots without beads for another 2in. (5cm).

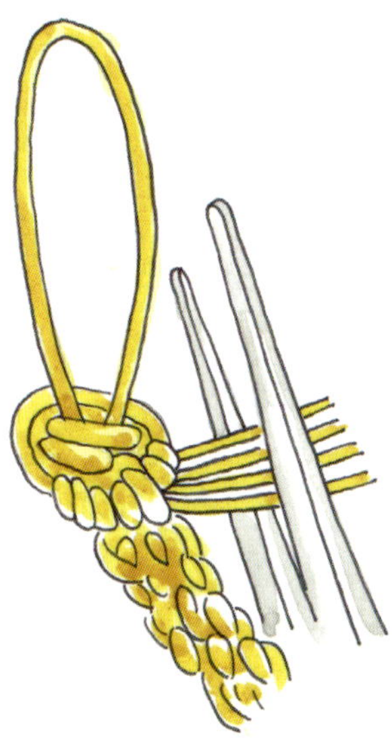

9 To finish, work a knot as above but tighten only some of the strands. The loop or loops that remain will become the fastening to go over the large bead. Tie a knot, trim the ends and seal with the lighter.

Green and orange alternative

Make the bracelet in exactly the same way except using four pieces of cord so each working cord is twice as thick. Instead of one beaded section, there are three smaller ones. This bracelet measures approximately 6in. (15cm).

Flower and nut clutch bag

I love the contrast of color and texture in this clutch bag. Make the piece of macramé first and then make a simple fabric bag to attach it to.

You will need

- 16in. (40cm) length of linen cord
- Thirty-two 80in. (200cm) lengths of linen cord
- Macramé board and pins
- Templates on page 140–141
- 24 x 12in. (60 x 30cm) of pink wool fabric
- 24 x 12in. (60 x 30cm) of patterned fabric
- Sewing machine and pink sewing thread
- Scissors
- Needle and thread

1 Stretch the short piece of linen cord across your macramé board and fix in place. Use lark's head knots (see page 7) to attach the 32 longer cords.

2 Working on the first pair of lark's head knots, use the center pair of strands as the filler cords and the outer pair as the working cords and work a square knot (see page 7). Repeat along the row with each pair of lark's head knots so you have a row of square knots.

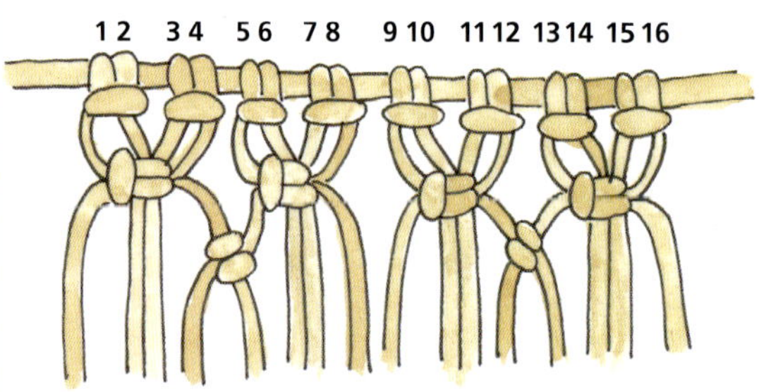

3 Arrange the cords in four batches of 16 to start working the flower petals. Beginning with the first batch, take cords 4 and 5 and work a clove hitch knot (see page 8), using cord 4 as the filler and cord 5 as the working cord. Skip the next six cords to the right and then work a reverse clove hitch knot (see page 8) using cord 13 as the filler cord and cord 12 as the working cord. Repeat this sequence on each batch along the row.

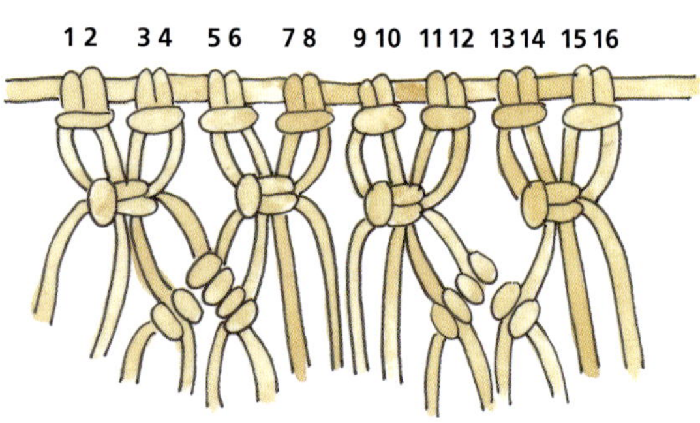

4 Use cord 3 to work a reverse clove hitch knot on cord 5. Use cord 7 to work a clove hitch knot on cord 4. Skip the next four cords and then work a reverse clove hitch knot on cord 13 using cord 11, and a clove hitch knot on cord 12 using cord 14. Repeat this sequence on each batch along the row.

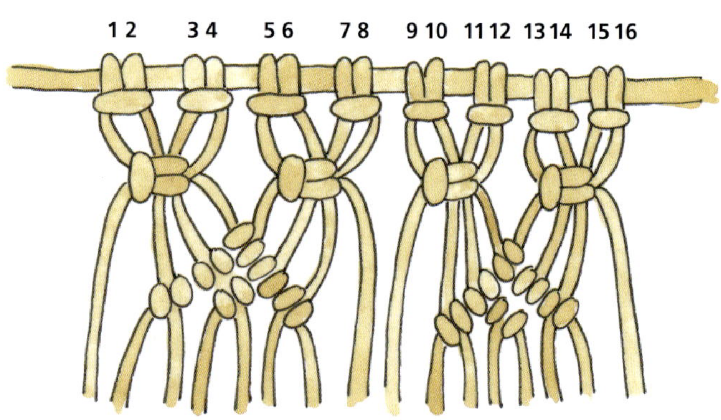

5 Use cord 2 to work a reverse clove hitch knot on cord 5. Use cord 3 to work a reverse clove hitch knot on cord 6. Use cord 7 to work a clove hitch knot on cord 4. Skip the next two cords and then work a reverse clove hitch knot on cord 13 using cord 10, a clove hitch knot on cord 11 using cord 14, and a clove hitch knot on cord 12 using cord 15. Repeat this sequence on each batch along the row.

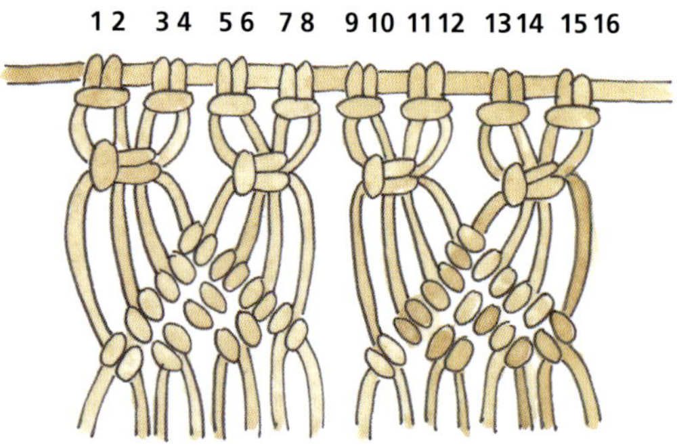

6 Use 5 to work a clove hitch knot on cord 1. Use cord 2 to work a reverse clove hitch knot on cord 6. Use cord 3 to work a reverse clove hitch knot on cord 7. Use cord 8 to work a clove hitch knot on cord 4. Then work a reverse clove hitch knot on cord 13 using cord 9, a clove hitch knot on cord 14 using cord 10, a clove hitch knot on cord 15 using cord 11, and a reverse clove hitch knot on cord 12 using cord 16. Repeat this sequence on each batch along the row.

7 Use cord 6 to work a clove hitch knot on cord 1. Use cord 2 to work a reverse clove hitch knot on cord 7. Use cord 3 to work a reverse clove hitch knot on cord 8. Skip the next two cords. Work a clove hitch knot on cord 9 using cord 14, work a clove hitch knot on cord 11 using cord 15, and work a reverse clove hitch knot on cord 16 using cord 11. Repeat this sequence on each batch along the row.

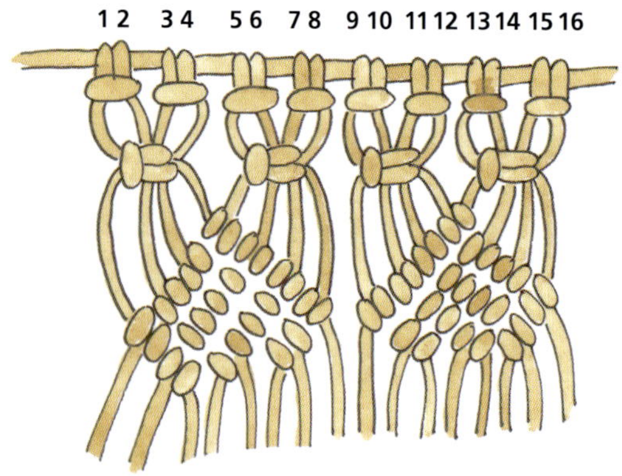

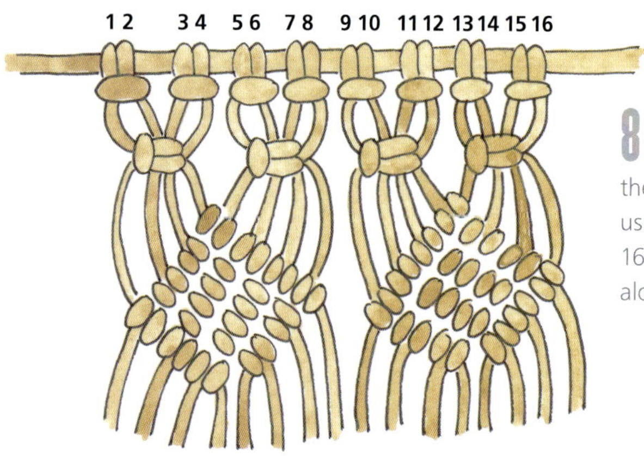

8 Now use cord 7 to work a clove hitch knot on cord 1, and cord 2 to work a reverse clove hitch knot on cord 8. Skip the next four cords. Work a clove hitch knot on cord 9 using cord 15 and work a reverse clove hitch knot on cord 16 using cord 10. Repeat this sequence on each batch along the row.

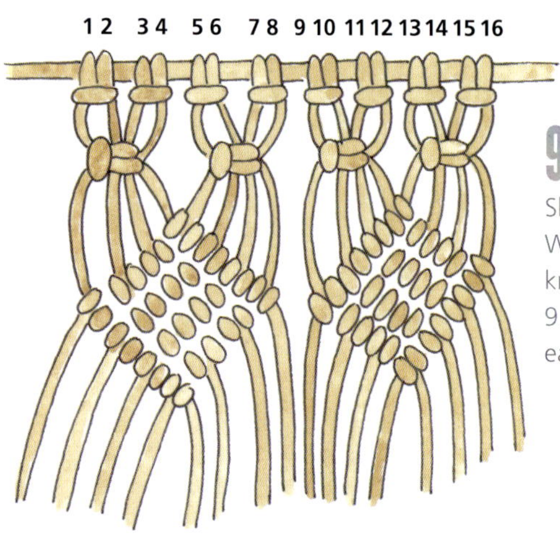

9 Take cord 8 and work a clove hitch knot on cord 1. Skip the next six cords. Work a reverse clove hitch knot on cord 16 using cord 9. Repeat this sequence on each batch along the row.

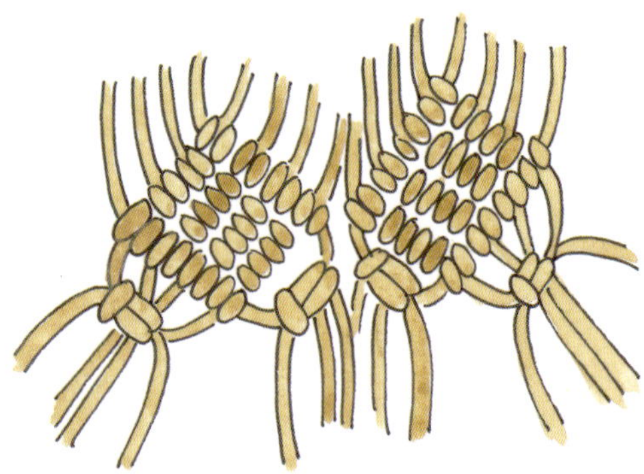

10 You will have four cords coming off on either side of each flower petal. Use each set of four to work a square knot to finish the petals.

11 Make the centers of the flowers by working three square knots using the two inner adjacent sets of four cords from the petals—eight cords in total, so the filler cords will be the six center cords and the working cords will be the two outer cords. Then thread the two outer cords up and through the hole at the top of the knots, from front to back.

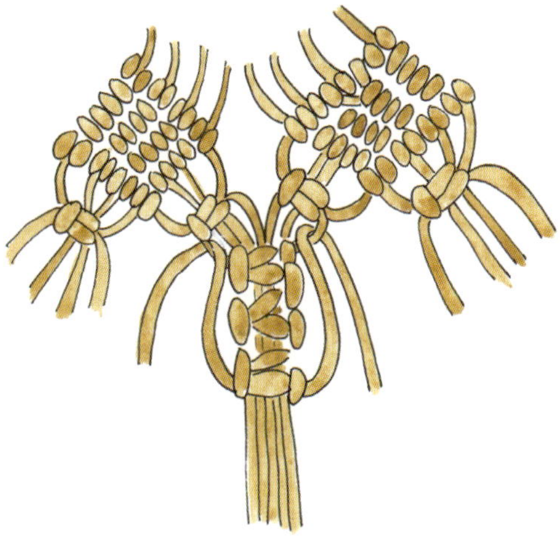

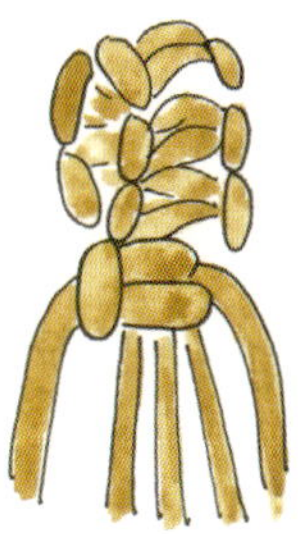

12 Pull tight, then work another square knot to secure in place. The flower center should puff up into a little bump.

13 Skip the next eight cords and then repeat steps 10–12 to make another petal center. Repeat along the row.

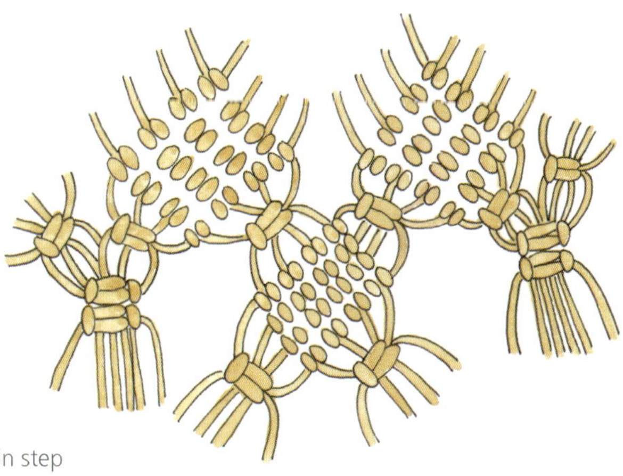

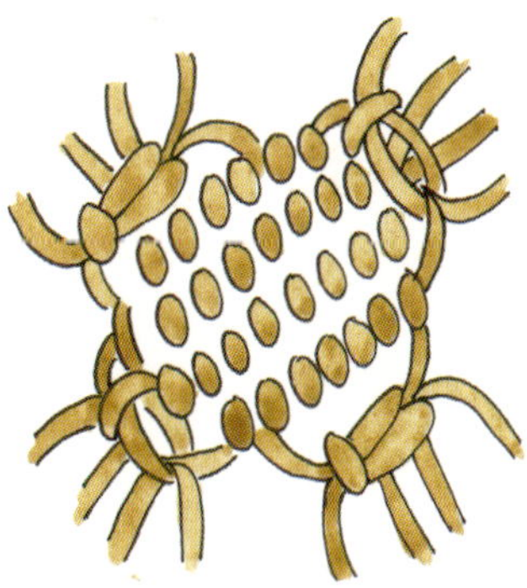

14 To make the nuts that nestle between the flowers, return to the outer sets of square knots on the petals made in step 10. Use two sets of adjacent cords (eight cords in total) to work rows of reverse clove hitch knots, using the cords on the right as the filler cords and the cords on the left as working cords. Complete by working a square knot with each set of four cords.

15 Tighten the square knots to puff up the nut into a bump.

16 Work a nut between each pair of flowers.

17 On row 3 make the lower set of petals by following steps 3 to 10, but flipping the direction of the knots so you work reverse clove hitch knots in place of all the clove hitch knots, and clove hitch knots in place of all the reverse clove hitch knots.

18 For row 4, skip four cords and then work a nut, flower center, nut, flower center, nut, flower center, and a nut.

19 On row 5, skip eight cords and then work steps 3 to 10 three times, but flipping the direction of the knots as in step 17.

20 For row 6, skip 12 cords and work a nut, flower center, nut, flower center, nut.

21 On row 7 skip 16 cords and work steps 3 to 10 twice, but flipping the direction of the knots as in steps 17 and 19.

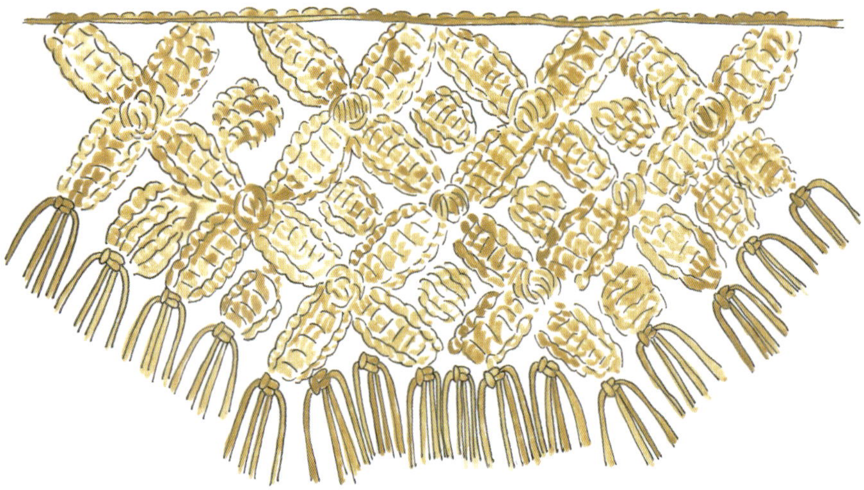

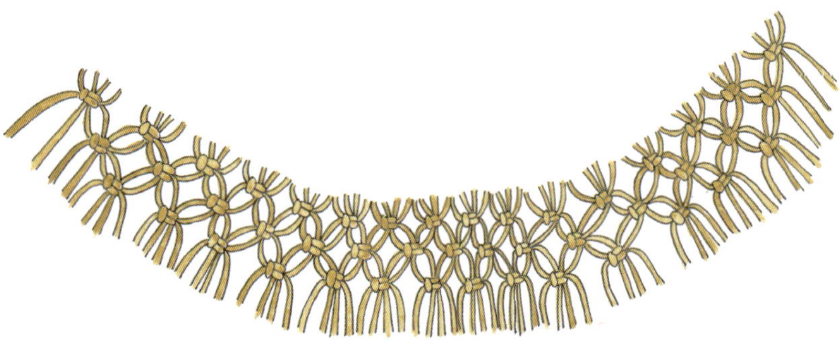

22 Finally, work two rows of square knots to complete the macramé section, dropping two cords at the start and end of both rows. Trim the cords to approximately 4in. (10cm).

23 Now make the bag. Use the templates on pages 140–141 to cut a Bag Lower Back, a Bag Flap, and a Bag Front from the pink fabric. Cut a Bag Back and a Bag Front from the patterned fabric.

24 Place the two patterned pieces right sides together as shown and machine stitch round the outer edge of the Bag Front, leaving a ⅜in. (1cm) seam allowance.

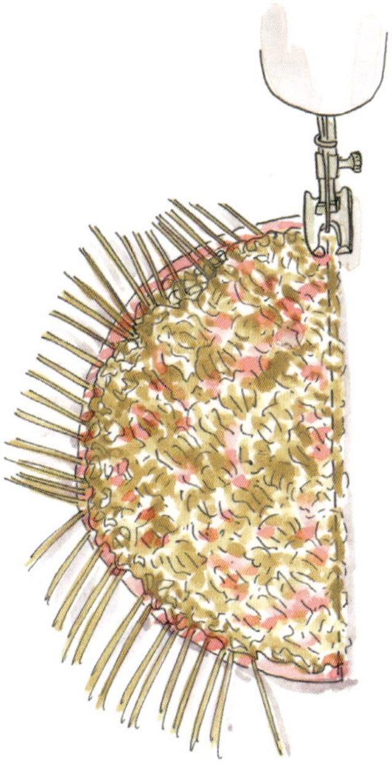

25 Sew the macramé piece to the right side of the Bag Flap using the sewing machine.

26 Place the Bag Flap and Bag Lower Back right sides together with the straight edge aligned. Sew the straight seam leaving a ⅜in. (1cm) seam allowance. Press the seam open.

27 Place the pink Bag Front right sides together onto the Bag Back made up in step 26, and sew round the outer edge of the Bag Front leaving a ⅜in. (1cm) seam allowance. Turn the pocket of the bag right side out.

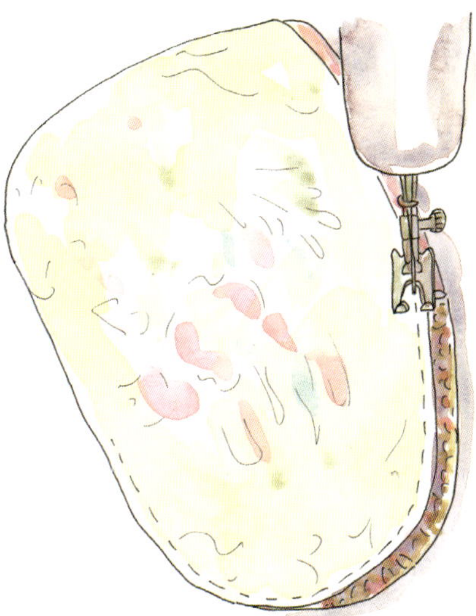

28 Place the macramé flap and the patterned flap pieces right sides together and sew around the Bag Flap only, leaving a ⅜in. (1cm) seam allowance. Ensure all the loose ends are tucked inside and don't get stitched.

29 Turn the flap right way out and push the floral lining inside the pink bag. Turn the raw edges along the top edge of the front to the inside and slipstitch together neatly.

Macramé rings

These delicate knotted rings are quickly and easily made using a very fine beading cord and working on ring blanks, which you can find online or in your local craft store.

You will need

- Cream, burnt orange, and green fine nylon beading cord
- 3 rose gold ring blanks with two holes
- Needle
- 3 orange seed beads
- 2 gold seed beads
- Scissors

Cream square knot ring

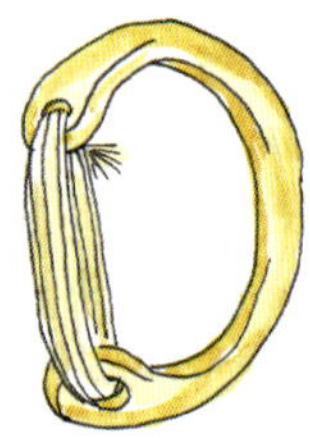

1 Cut a piece of cream cord 12in. (30cm) long and thread around and through the holes in the ring four times. Tie the ends in a knot and trim. This is the core or the filler cords for your ring design.

2 Cut two pieces of cream cord 24in. (60cm) and tie to the top of the filler cords. Work square knots (see page 7) all along the length of the filler cords, pushing the knots closely and tightly together as you work.

3 Thread the cord ends up through the knots and trim to secure.

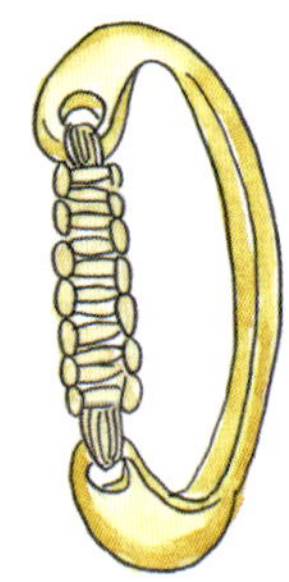

Alternating knot ring

1 Repeat step 1 as for the Cream Square Knot Ring.

2 Cut a 24in. (60cm) length of each of the green and burnt orange cords, fold in half and tie to the top of the filler cords. Take the two green cord ends and work a backward knot (see page 6). Then take the two orange cord ends and work a forward knot (see page 6). Repeat along the length of the filler cords.

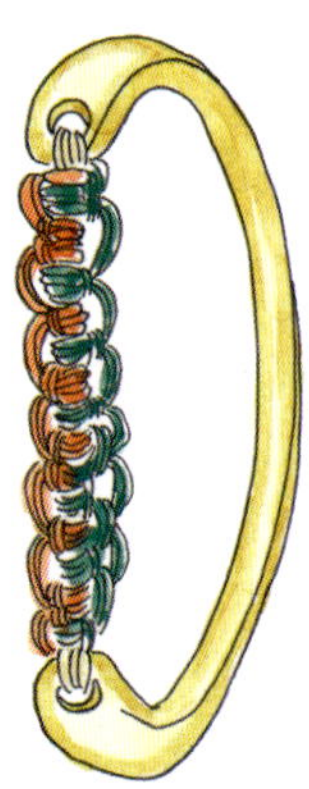

3 Thread the cord ends up through the knots and trim to secure.

Beaded ring

1 Repeat step 1 as for the Cream Square Knot Ring, but thread the orange and gold seed beads alternately onto the cord as you thread it through the holes on the ring.

2 Cut a 24in. (60cm) length of cream cord and tie it to the top of the filler cords. Work square knots between each bead to secure in place.

3 Thread the cord ends up through the knots and trim to secure.

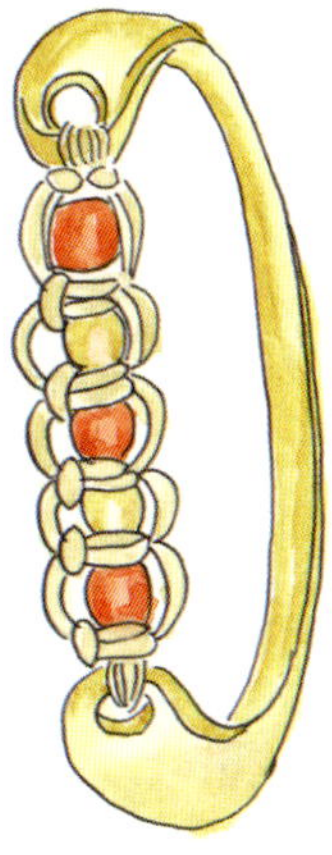

Chunky rope necklace

The ultimate statement necklace. People won't believe when you say you made this—it's such a dramatic piece!

You will need

- 20in. (50cm) of 0.5cm diameter rope
- Macramé board and pins
- Twelve 120in. (300cm) lengths of 0.5cm diameter rope
- Six 80in. (200cm) lengths of 0.5cm diameter rope
- Scissors
- Needle and thread

1 Stretch the 20in. (50cm) cord along the top of your macramé board as an anchor cord and attach the twelve 120in. (300cm) cords using lark's head knots (see page 7).

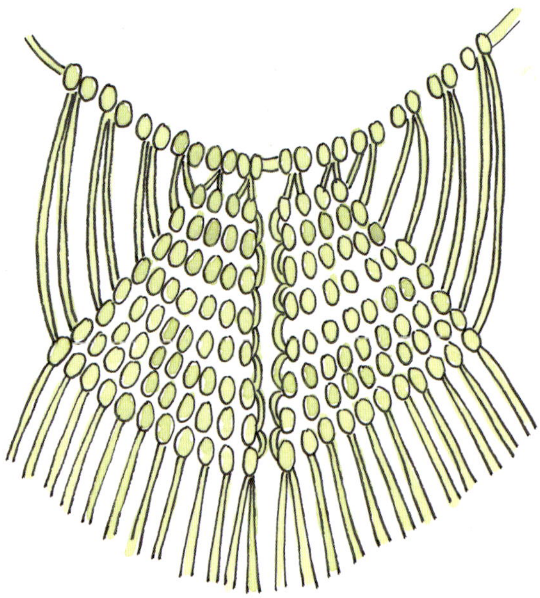

2 Start making the first panels, working in rows:

Row 1: Take the eighth cord from the left-hand side and use it to work four forward knots (see page 6) over cords 9, 10, 11, and 12.

Row 2: Take the seventh cord from the left-hand side and use it to work five forward knots over cords 9, 10, 11, 12, and 8.

Row 3: Take the sixth cord from the left-hand side and use it to work six forward knots over cords 9, 10, 11, 12, 8, and 7.

Row 4: Take the fifth cord from the left-hand side and use it to work seven forward knots over cords 9, 10, 11, 12, 8, 7, and 6.

Row 5: Take the fourth cord from the left-hand side and use it to work eight forward knots over cords 9, 10, 11, 12, 8, 7, 6, and 5.

Row 6: Take the third cord from the left-hand side and use it to work nine forward knots over cords 9, 10, 11, 12, 8, 7, 6, 5, and 4.

Row 7: Take the second cord from the left-hand side and use it to work ten forward knots over cords 9, 10, 11, 12, 8, 7, 6, 4, 5, and 3.

Row 8: Take the first cord on the left-hand side and use it to work eleven forward knots over cords 9, 10, 11, 12, 8, 7, 6, 5, 4, 3, and 2.

Repeat, working from the right-hand side using backward knots (see page 6).

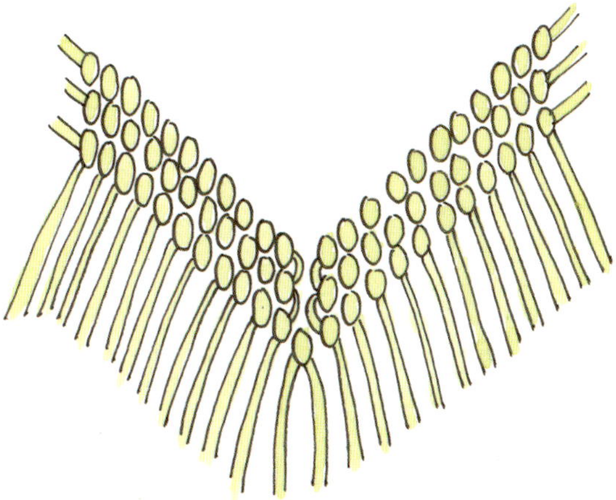

3 Tie a forward knot using the two central cords to join the two panels of braiding.

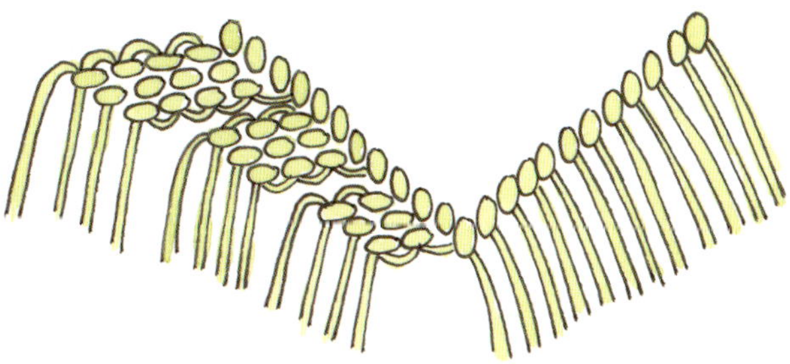

4 **Rows 9–12**: Working from the left-hand side again, use cord 4 to work three backward knots on cords 3, 2, and 1. Work another three rows using these cords. Then use cord 8 to work three backward knots on cords 7, 6, and 5. Work another two rows using these cords. Use cord 12 to work three backward knots on cords 11, 10, and 9.

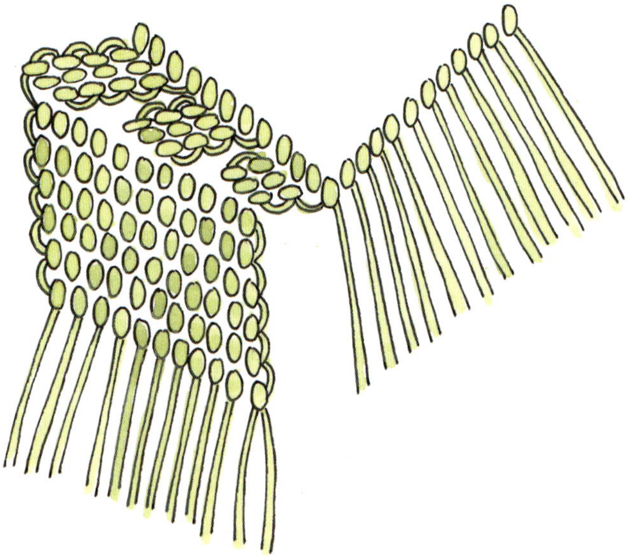

5 Rows 13–18: Again starting from the left-hand side, using all the cords from 1 to 12 in order and working across from left to right, make six rows of forward knots.

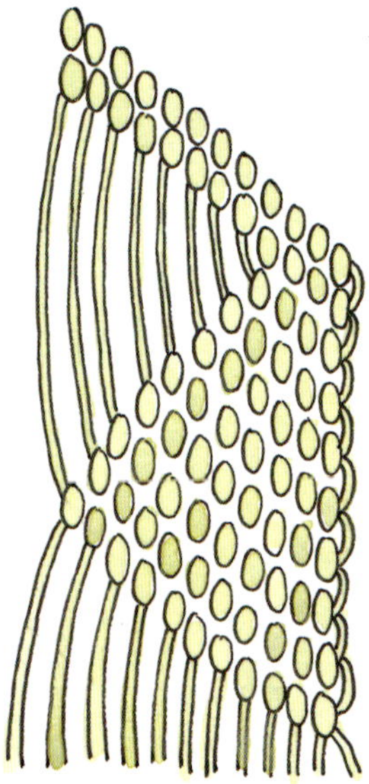

6 Rows 19–26: Go back to cord 8 on the left-hand side and work four forward knots over cords 9, 10, 11, and 12. Use cord 7 to work five forward knots over cords 9, 10, 11, 12, and 8. Continue in the same way with cords 6 to 1, increasing the number of forward knots by one each time.

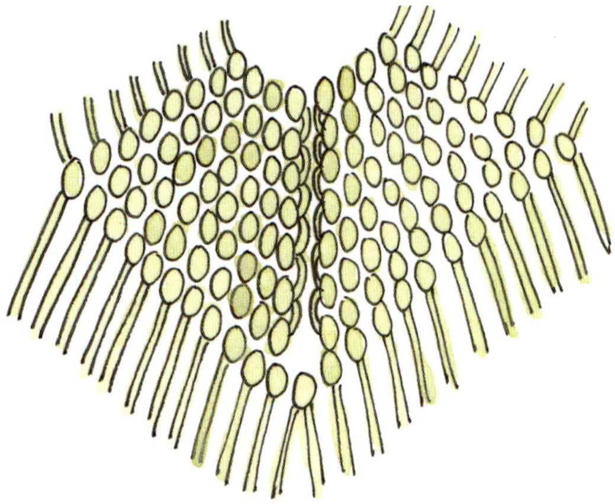

7 Repeat steps 4–6 on the right-hand side, using forward knots for step 4 and backward knots for steps 5 and 6. Join the two panels with a forward knot using the central two cords.

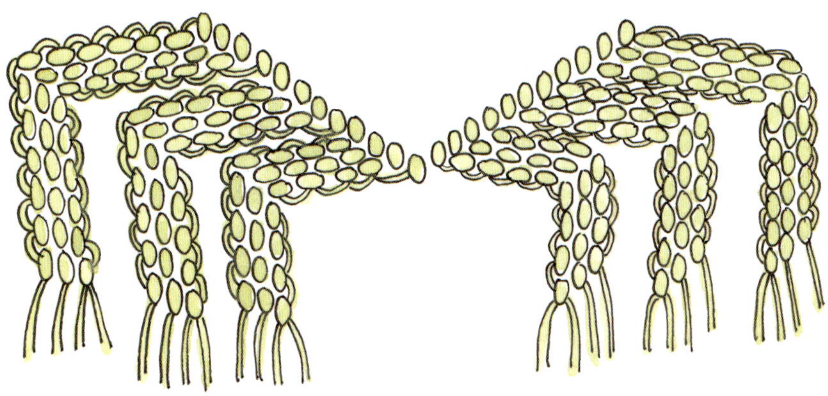

8 Rows 27–32: Use cord 4 to work three backward knots on cords 3, 2, and 1. Work another five rows using these cords. Use cord 8 to work three backward knots on cords 7, 6, and 5. Work another four rows with these cords. Use cord 12 to work three backward knots on cords 11, 10, and 9. Work another three rows with these cords. Repeat this sequence on the right-hand side, using forward knots.

9 Rows 33–38: Use cord 1 to work three forward knots on cords 2, 3, and 4. Work another five rows using these cords. Use cord 5 to work three backward knots on cords 6, 7, and 8. Work another four rows with these cords. Use cord 9 to work three backward knots on cords 10, 11, and 12. Work another three rows with these cords. Repeat this sequence on the right-hand side, using backward knots.

10 Now work six rows of forward knots from the left and backward knots from the right, joining each row with a forward knot using the center two cords before moving onto the next row.

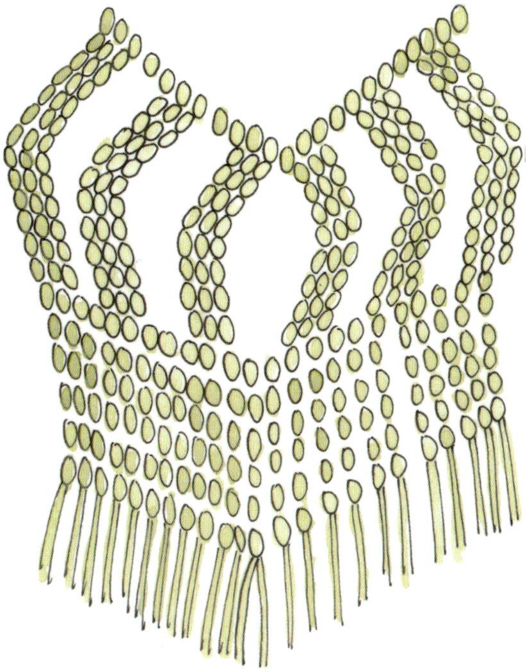

11 Trim the cord ends to 6in. (15cm).

12 Fold three of the 80in. (2m) cords in half and attach them to the anchor cord just to the left of the original cords using lark's head knots. Repeat on the right with the other three cords.

13 Starting on the left set, work 45 rows of clove hitch knots (see page 8) working from left to right. Repeat on the right side, working reverse clove hitch knots (see page 8) from right to left.

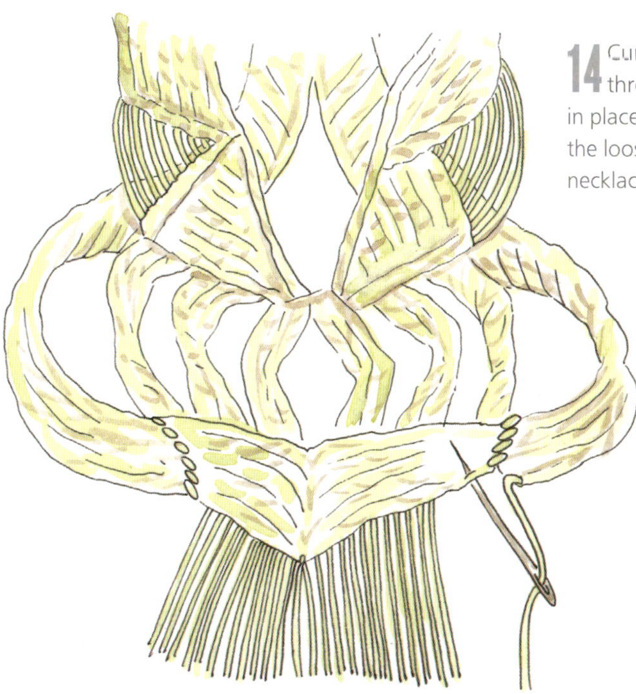

14 Curl the pieces just made as shown, threading through and stitching in place as required, and then sewing the loose ends neatly into the main necklace at the base of each side.

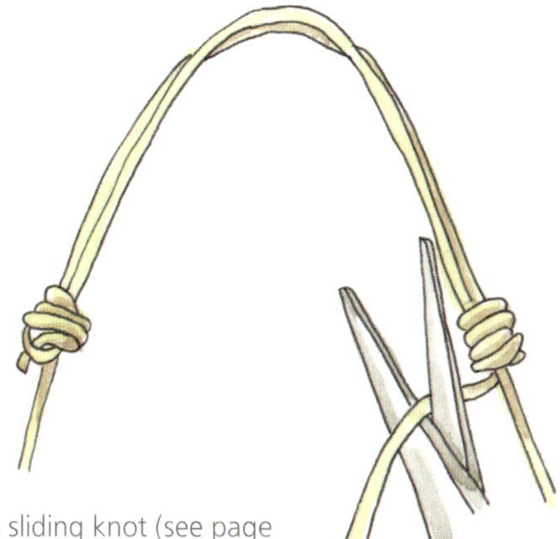

15 Tie a sliding knot (see page 8) on the anchor cords to complete the necklace.

Ribbon necklace and bracelet

This necklace and bangle set look incredible, but they are such fun and easy to make.

You will need

- 200in. (500cm) of lime green ribbon
- 200in. (500cm) of yellow ribbon
- 200in. (500cm) of turquoise ribbon
- 200in. (500cm) of blue ribbon
- Two 35mm ribbon clasps
- Pliers
- Two 12in. (30cm) lengths of chain
- 4 jump rings
- Lobster claw clasp
- 160in. (400cm) of pink ribbon
- 160in. (400cm) of orange ribbon
- Scissors

1 Fold both the green and yellow ribbons in half and tie together in a knot just below the loop.

2 Fold the green ribbons over in opposite directions so they lie side by side, over the yellow ribbons running upward and downward.

3 Take the upper yellow ribbon end and thread it over and under the green ribbons.

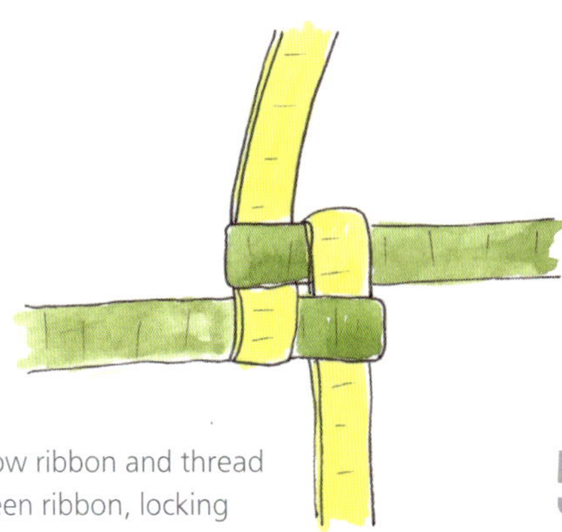

4 Then take the lower yellow ribbon and thread it over and under the green ribbon, locking all the ribbons in place.

5 Repeat steps 2–4 until your braid measures approximately 12in. (30cm). Then repeat steps 1–5 using the turquoise and blue ribbons.

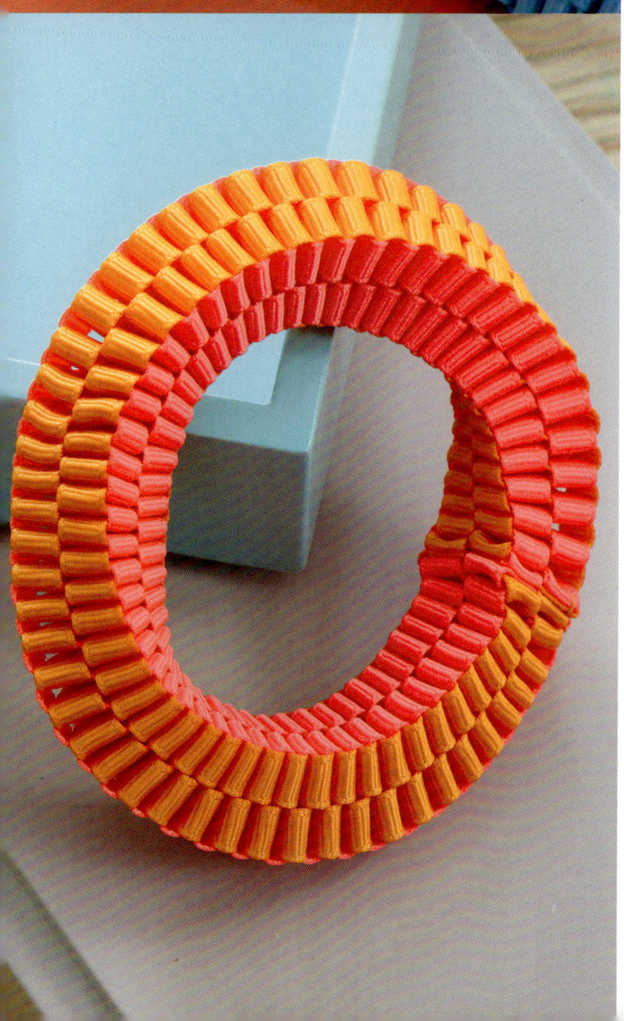

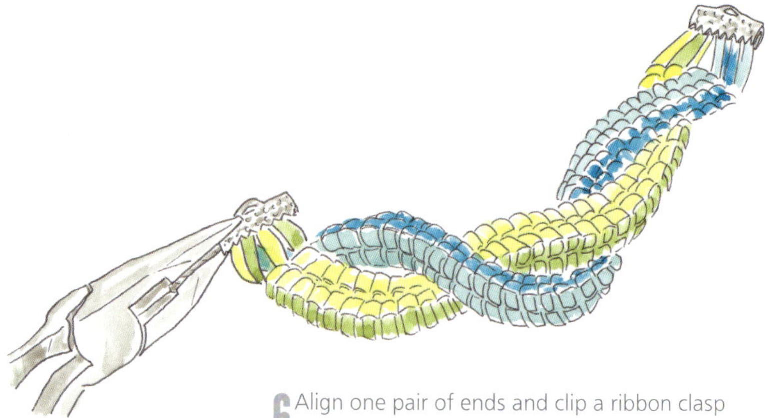

6 Align one pair of ends and clip a ribbon clasp on to hold them together, using pliers. Twist the two braids together, and then add the second ribbon clasp on the other set of ends.

7 Attach a length of chain to each ribbon clasp with a jump ring, again using pliers.

8 Attach a jump ring to one end of the chain and a lobster claw clasp to the other, again using a jump ring.

9 To make the bracelet, repeat steps 1–5 using the pink and orange ribbons—the braid will be only approximately 6in. (15cm) long because the ribbons are shorter. Sew the ends together to create a bangle shape.

Macramé bead ring

Work knots around a felt ball to make a macramé bead, and then make this into a chunky ring.

You will need

- Eight 40in. (100cm) lengths of stranded cotton floss in each of blue, cream, and yellow
- Sixteen 40in. (100cm) lengths of lime green stranded cotton floss
- ¾in. (2cm) felt ball
- Macramé board and pins
- 200in. (500cm) of orange stranded cotton floss
- Scissors
- Ring blank
- Superglue

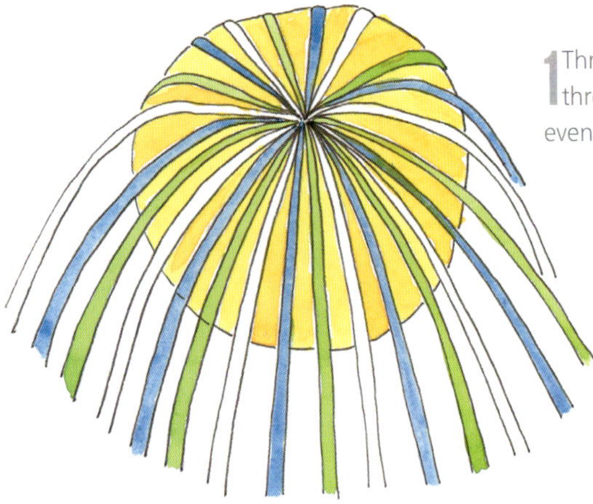

1 Thread eight blue, eight cream, and eight lime green threads through the center of the felt ball and arrange evenly around in sequence as shown.

2 Pin the ball to the board and then pin the orange thread to the ball over where the threads emerge. Work clove hitch knots (see page 8) on the orange thread, starting with the green thread and working all around the ball.

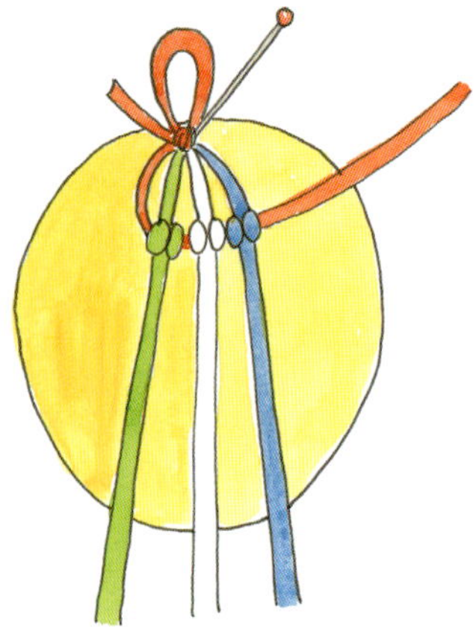

3 **Row 2**: Repeat step 2.

4 **Row 3**: Work a forward knot (see page 6) with the orange thread on the green thread, then work two clove hitch knots on the orange thread using the cream and blue threads. Repeat around the ball.

5 **Row 4**: Work a forward knot with the orange thread on the green thread, then work a clove hitch knot on the orange thread using the cream. Attach a green thread to the orange thread using a lark's head knot (see page 7), and then make a clove hitch knot with the blue thread on the orange thread. Repeat around the ball.

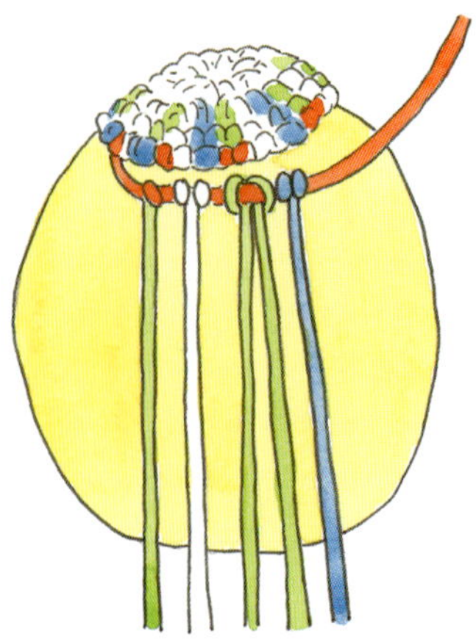

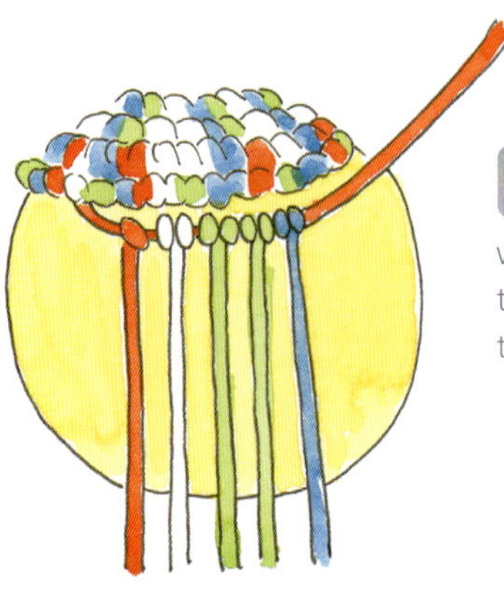

6 **Row 5**: Work a forward knot with the orange thread on the green thread, then work four clove hitch knots on the orange thread using the cream, the two green threads, and the blue. Repeat around the ball.

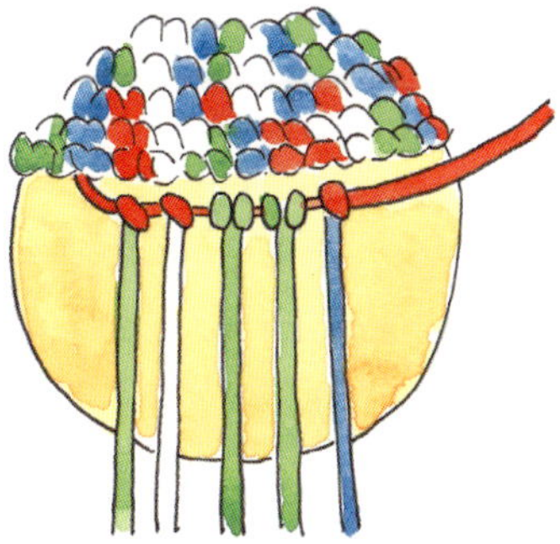

7 Row 6: Work two forward knots with the orange thread on the green and cream threads, then work two clove hitch knots on the orange thread using the two green threads, then work another forward knot using the orange thread on the blue thread. Repeat around the ball.

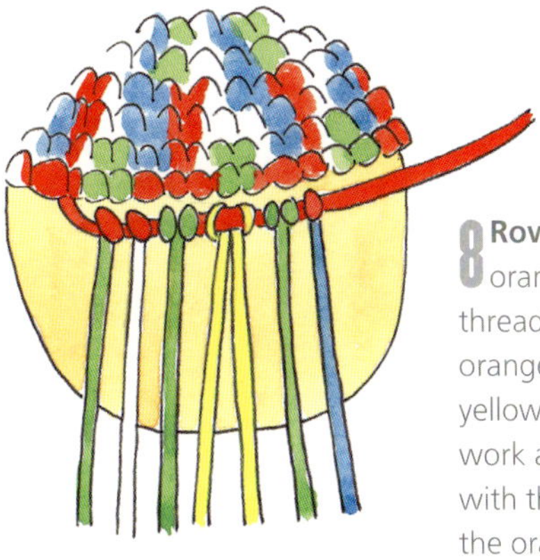

8 Row 7: Work two forward knots with the orange thread on the green and cream threads, then work a clove hitch knot on the orange thread using a green thread. Attach a yellow cord using a lark's head knot, and then work a clove hitch knot on the orange thread with the green thread and a forward knot with the orange thread on the blue thread. Repeat around the ball.

9 Row 8: Work two forward knots with the orange thread on the green and cream threads, then work four clove hitch knots on the orange thread using the green, two yellow threads, and the green thread, and then a forward knot using the orange thread on the blue thread. Repeat around the ball.

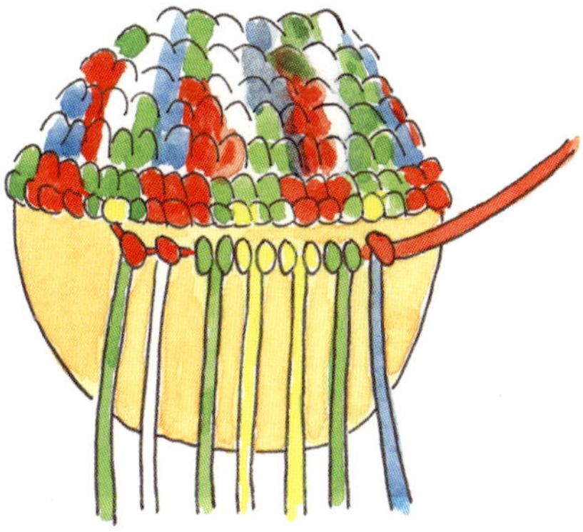

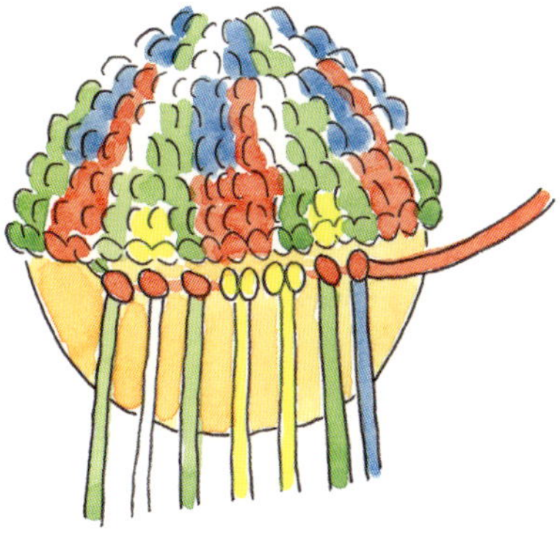

10 Row 9: Work three forward knots with the orange thread on the green, cream, and green threads, two clove hitch knots using the two yellow threads on the orange thread, and then two forward knots using the orange thread on the green and blue threads. Repeat around the ball.

11 Now start reducing the rows. Repeat steps 9 to 3 in reverse, skipping the cords that were added and leaving them loose at the back of the braiding.

12 At the end, push all the thread ends back up into the ball and trim. Stick the ball to the ring blank using superglue. Allow to dry before wearing.

Leather and wool cuff

Combine metallic leather and rustic wool in this cool cuff. Use a simple spiraling half square knot to create this effect.

You will need

- Template on page 141
- 1¾ x 8in. (4.5 x 20cm) piece of silver leather
- Craft knife
- Cutting board
- 160in. (400cm) of aqua wool
- 160in. (400cm) of dusky pink wool
- 160in. (400cm) of mustard wool
- Scissors
- 2 metal snap fasteners

1 Using the template on page 141, cut four slots into the piece of leather using your craft knife.

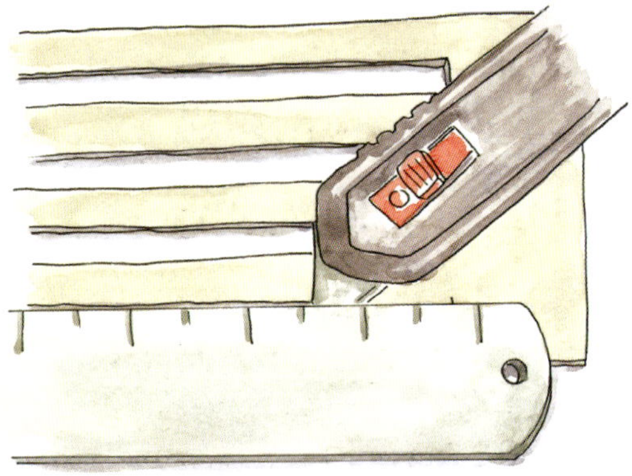

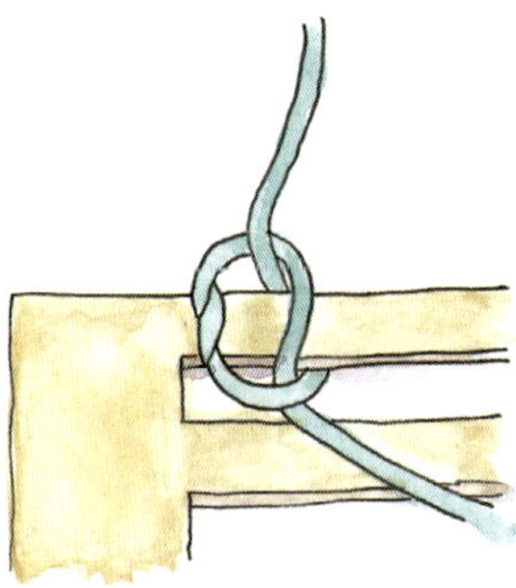

2 Tie one end of the aqua wool to the right-hand end of the first bar. Work a left facing half square knot (see page 8).

3 Repeat the half square knots until the whole bar is covered. Keep pushing the knots up tightly so they cover the leather.

4 Trim any excess yarn and thread the end back up through the braid to secure.

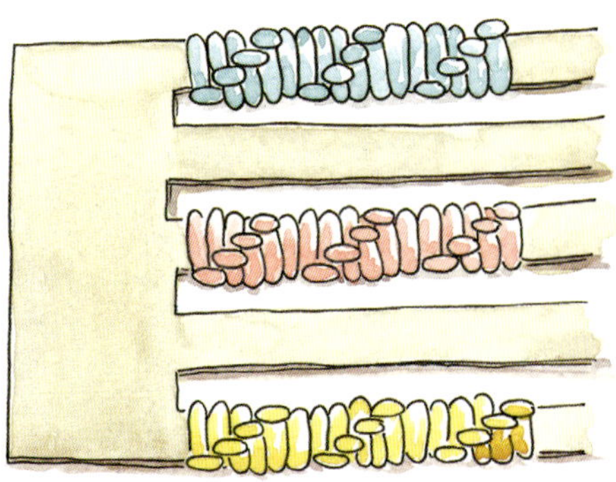

5 Repeat steps 2–4 with the pink and mustard yarns along the next two bars.

6 Following the instructions on the packet, attach the snap fasteners to the cuff ends to complete.

Barbed wire elastic bracelet

You will need

- 40in. (1m) each of ¼in. (5mm) elastic in silver and gold
- Macramé board and pins
- Two ¼in. (5mm) ribbon clamps
- Pliers
- Lobster claw clasp
- 4 silver jump rings
- Scissors

Rather than thread or cord, this bracelet is made using metallic elastic and looks rather like barbed wire!

1 Place the two lengths of elastic together, fold in half and tie a knot 2in. (5cm) from the looped end. Pin the knot to your macramé board.

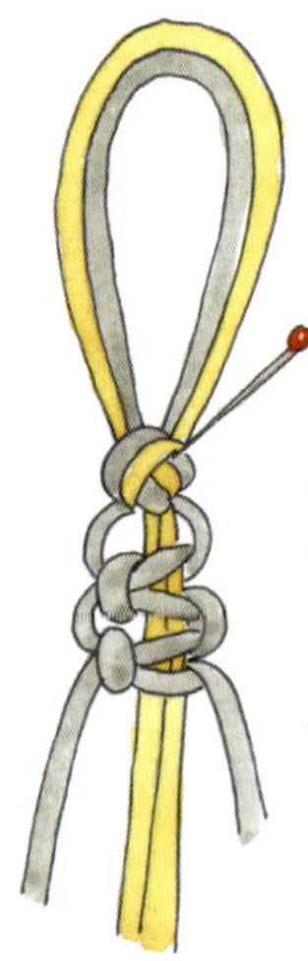

2 Work two square knots (see page 7) using the two strands of silver elastic, with the two strands of gold elastic as the filler cords.

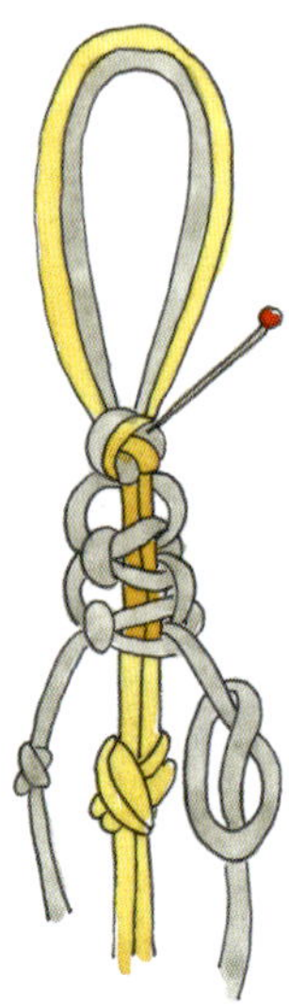

3 Tie a knot in each of the silver outer cords and knot the two gold cords together.

4 Repeat steps 2 and 3 until your bracelet measures 6in. (15cm).

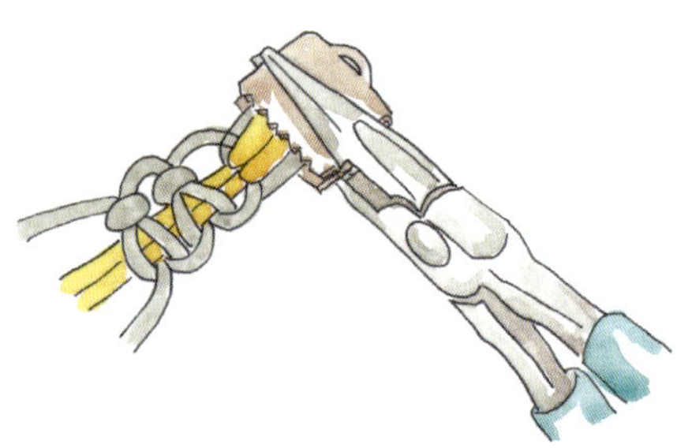

5 Trim both sets of ends to ½in. (1cm). Use the pliers to attach a ribbon clamp to each end.

6 Using pliers, add the lobster claw clasp to one ribbon clamp and a few jump rings to the other.

Templates

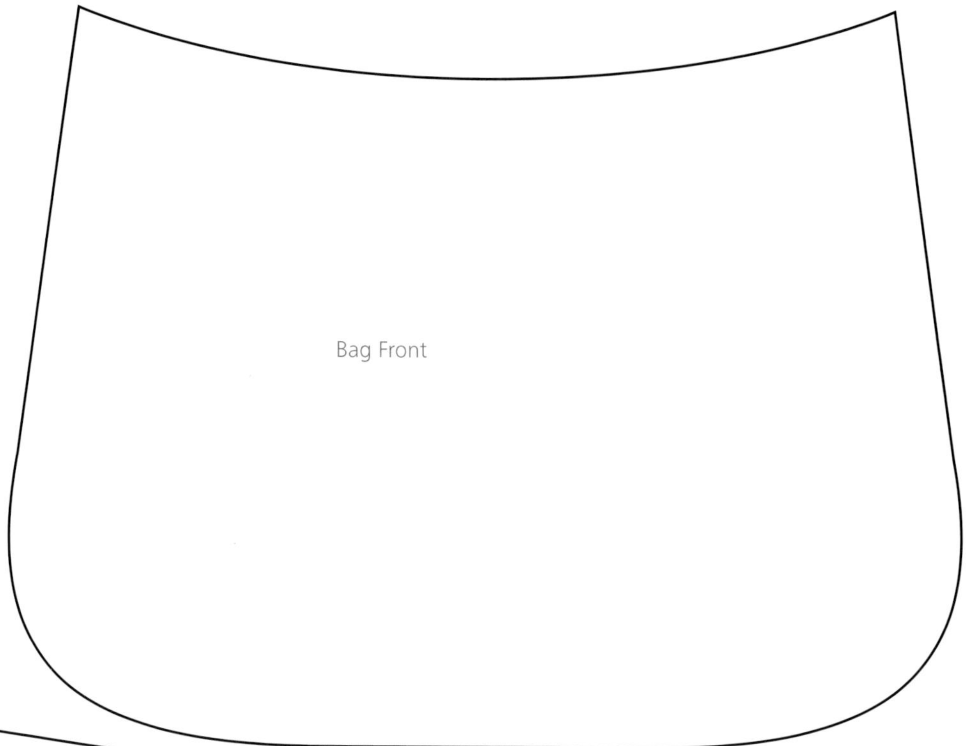

Flower and Nut Clutch Bag page 118

These templates are printed at 50%: they will need to be enlarged by 200% using a photocopier.

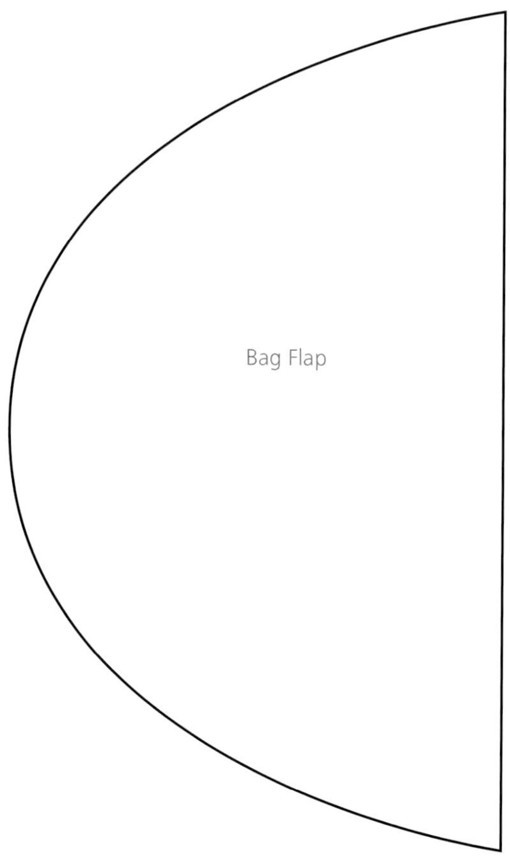

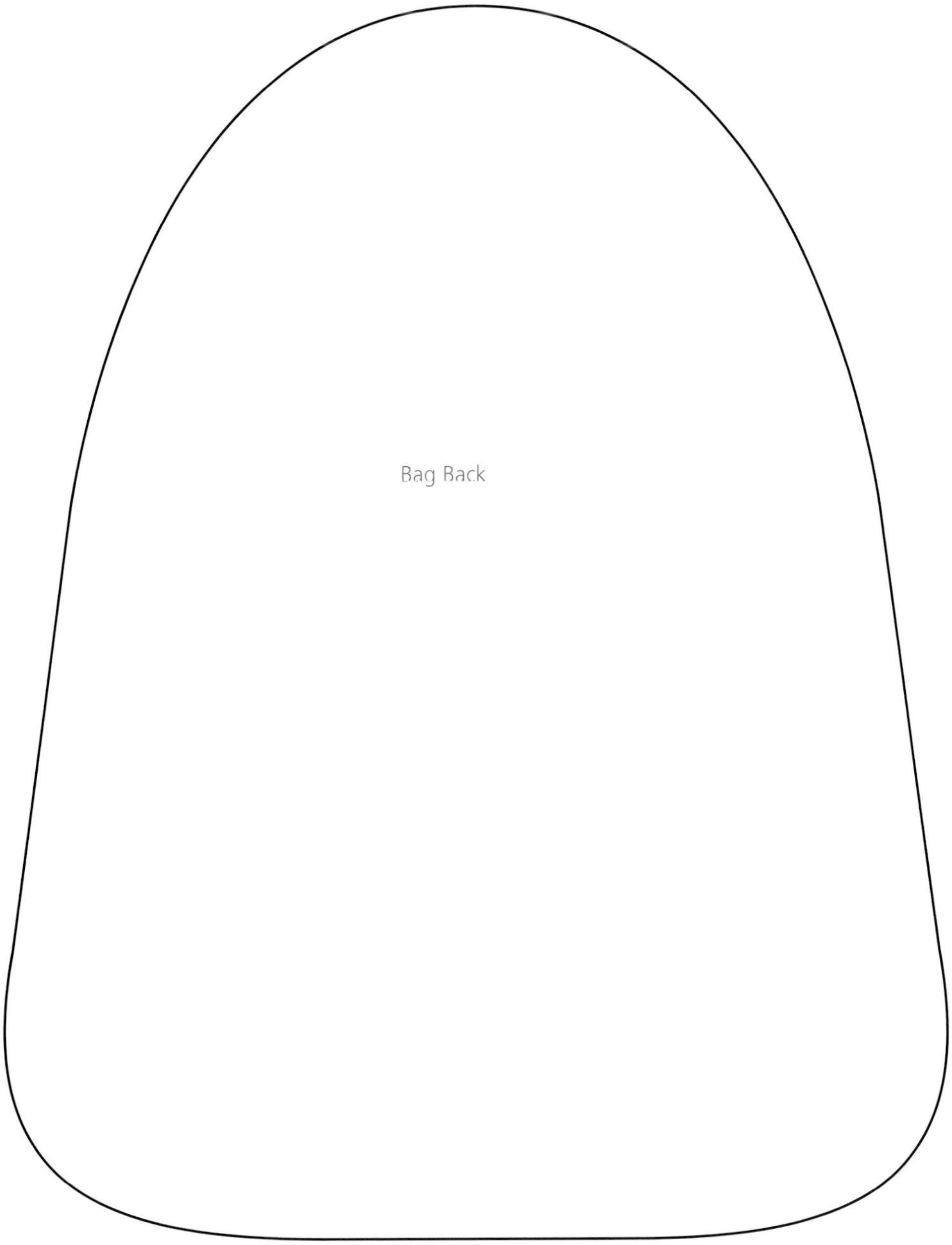

Leather and Wool Cuff page 136

This template is printed at actual size—no need to enlarge

Suppliers

North America

Britex Fabrics
www.britexfabrics.com

Buy Fabrics
www.buyfabrics.com

Charm Factory
www.charmfactory.com

Fabricland
www.fabricland.com

Hobby Lobby
www.hobbylobby.com

JOANN
www.joann.com

Michaels
www.michaels.com

Walmart
www.walmart.com

United Kingdom

Abakhan Fabrics
www.abakhan.co.uk

Beads Direct Ltd
www.beadsdirect.co.uk

The Bead Shop
www.the-beadshop.co.uk

Beads Unlimited
www.beadsunlimited.co.uk

Hobbycraft
www.hobbycraft.co.uk

Homebase
www.homebase.co.uk

Jasmin Studio Crafts
www.jasminstudiocrafts.com

John Lewis
www.johnlewis.com

Liberty
www.libertylondon.com

Index

Acknowledgments

As ever I would like to thank all those at CICO for creating yet another stunning book. Particular mention must go to the editors Anna Galkina and Marie Clayton and the Illustrator Louise Turpin, who all struggled through my copy and rough sketches and miraculously turned them into concise instructions and beautiful illustrations. I think all the late night emails, illustration checks, and burning eyes from knotting into the early hours were worth it!

I must also thank my family for helping me with childcare. Writing a book with a 6-month-old is a whole different ball game to writing with a newborn! Thank you Mum, Dad, Clare, Richard, Sue, Malc, and of course my husband Jamie for helping me when the deadlines loomed!